KT-244-758

COLLECTOR'S GUIDE TO
ANTIQUE PORCELAIN

Westerners Shopping for Porcelain
Chinese Export plate, c. 1725–1740
(*Courtesy The Henry Francis du Pont*
Winterthur Museum,
Winterthur, Delaware)

Gordon A. Rust

ANDRE DEUTSCH

Collector's Guide to
ANTIQUE
PORCELAIN

TITLE PAGE:
"Hong" Bowl
Chinese Export, early nineteenth century
Decoration: Polychrome scene of
foreign "Hongs" at Canton
(*Courtesy Diplomatic Reception Rooms,*
U. S. Department of State,
Washington, D. C.)

RIGHT: Chinese Figure
Vezzi (Italian), *c.* 1723
Venice
Decoration: Polychrome—red, yellow, blue, green
(*Courtesy The Metropolitan Museum of Art,*
New York, New York.
Gift of R. Thornton Wilson, 1950,
in memory of Florence Ellsworth Wilson)

OPPOSITE PAGE: Plate
Chinese Export, *c.* 1800
Decoration: Orange Fitzhugh pattern
with sepia American eagle
(*Courtesy Diplomatic Reception Rooms,*
U. S. Department of State,
Washington, D. C.,
with the permission of The Dietrich Foundation, Inc.)

For Frances

First published 1973 by
André Deutsch Ltd.
105 Great Russell Street
London W C 1
Copyright © 1973 by Gordon A. Rust
All rights reserved
Colour Illustrations. Printed in Japan
Text and Black and White Illustrations.
Printed in U.S.A.
ISBN 0 233 96489 4

CONTENTS

A COLLECTOR'S CHOICE   11
THE APPEALS OF PORCELAIN   13
HARD- AND SOFT-PASTE PORCELAIN   15
CHINESE PORCELAIN   19
PORCELAIN AND THE CHINA TRADE   26
CHINESE EXPORT PORCELAIN:
  A DESIGN CHECKLIST   31
JAPANESE PORCELAINS   41
THE IDENTIFICATION OF ANTIQUE
  PORCELAIN   48
THE DECORATION OF PORCELAIN   106
MAJOR PORCELAIN FACTORIES   108
APPENDIXES   126
  CHRONOLOGY   126
  GLOSSARY   129
  BIBLIOGRAPHY   136
  PUBLIC COLLECTIONS OF ANTIQUE
    PORCELAIN   142

Acknowledgments

I am particularly indebted to two professionals in the field of antique porcelain: Mr. J. Jefferson Miller II, Curator of Ceramics History at the Smithsonian Institution in Washington, D.C., and Mr. Dwight Lanmon, Curator of Ceramics and Glass at the Henry Francis du Pont Winterthur Museum in Delaware. Both Mr. Miller and Mr. Lanmon have generously taken the time to read the text of this book, and both have provided invaluable guidance. Curators in many other museums have also been most helpful.

I also owe much to the many dealers in antique porcelain, in America and Europe, who have so patiently contributed to my education, whether I was buying or not. I have benefited greatly from their knowledge and experience.

Finally, I am indebted to Mrs. Randolph Barton, Jr., who, for a porcelain loan exhibit at the Delaware Antiques Show, painted on tile the porcelain marks appearing here; and to Miss Wendy Cooper, Assistant Curator at the Brooklyn Museum, who, with great expertise, read the text for errors and omissions.

PREFACE

The purpose of the *Collector's Guide to Antique Porcelain* is to provide a concise, introductory reference book in the field of antique porcelain, from its origins to about 1825.

Many exhaustive and authoritative volumes, handsomely printed and illustrated, are available for nearly every major porcelain factory. Such volumes of specialized reference are indispensable to the advanced collector.

The beginning student of antique porcelain, as well as the new collector, needs rather different assistance, namely, a book of fundamental facts and guidance covering the entire subject simply and briefly.

It is hoped that this *Collector's Guide to Antique Porcelain* will fill this need in a helpful, comprehensive, and reliable fashion.

Gordon A. Rust

"FAIR HILL"
Mendenhall, Pennsylvania

Octagonal Bowl, Arita Ware (Kakiemon Type)
Japanese, late seventeenth–early eighteenth century
Decoration: Polychrome enamels
(*Courtesy The St. Louis Art Museum,*
St. Louis, Missouri.
W. K. Bixby Oriental Art Fund
and gift of Mr. and Mrs. Arthur B. Baer)

THE HONGS OF CANTON, CHINNERY SCHOOL, *c.* 1845

Most Chinese "Export" porcelains which reached the outside world in the
eighteenth and nineteenth centuries began their journey in this narrow enclave

of "Hongs" or "factories" at Canton, China, two names often used to mean porcelain. The Hong buildings were leased for the annual trading season to merchants representing, in some years, as many as a dozen foreign countries. It was the superb porcelain of China (and Japan), brought home by earlier traders, that so inspired the potters of Europe. (*From the author's collection*)

A COLLECTOR'S CHOICE

As the prices of eighteenth-century and other antique porcelains increase with every sale and auction, the newly interested collector could well be discouraged from adopting such an expensive hobby. It is true that the rarest porcelains are now beyond the reach of all but the most affluent individuals and museums. Yet with imagination, knowledge, and perseverance it is still possible to build a collection of genuine quality at reasonable prices.

Some years ago, with an interest whetted by residence and travel in the Orient, the author hit upon his own solution—the selection of a single shape that was at once modest and common to many nations, periods, and factories. This was the cylindrical shape of the tankard or mug, sometimes also called a coffee cann by the English. Adults and children alike drank all kinds of liquid refreshment from this useful object. Moreover, the tankard, modeled after its counterparts in silver, pewter, and pottery, was produced in enormous quantities and so is more readily and reasonably available today. Lacking, of course, the great artistry, elegance, and variety of porcelain sculptures and other purely decorative designs, the tankard nevertheless illustrates all the variations in paste, decoration, and other detail that, taken in continuity, tell the story of porcelain.

Many other choices can be made as the basis of new collections: particular shapes, periods, factories, and decorative influences. From these, one can derive nearly the same interest and reward as from the rarest porcelains. One collector may be drawn to heraldry, another to botanical, theatrical, nautical, or even sporting subjects. Whatever direction one takes, and collecting should never be aimless, it is reassuring to remember that the steady proliferation of private and public collections almost certainly guarantees that one's investment will over the years increase in value—just as it is doing today in nearly every area of the fine arts.

So don't be dismayed by the scarcity and the price of fine antique porcelain. It is still possible to collect wisely and well if one is guided by a few basic rules. It is hoped that this book will provide such a frame of reference.

White Figure, Küan Yin
Chinese (Ming), 1368–1644
(*Courtesy Nelson Gallery—Atkins Museum,
Kansas City, Missouri.
Nelson Fund*)

11

Jug
Worcester (English), *c.* 1765
Decoration: Canary yellow ground
with Chinese landscape in
enamel colors and gilt
(*Courtesy The Metropolitan
Museum of Art, New York, New York.
Gift of Mr. and Mrs. Luke Vincent Lockwood, 1939*)

THE APPEALS OF PORCELAIN

At first glance, the subject of antique porcelain might appear to have only a special and limited appeal—chiefly for the connoisseur of the rare and the beautiful. A closer study, however, reveals a story with an amazing range of appeals. We find the mystery of a suspense tale, since for centuries the Chinese concealed the very secret of porcelain. Missionaries, traders, and other travelers all tried in vain to discover the formula. As the European demand for porcelain grew to almost manic proportions, the great seafaring countries found their way to China, with all the hazard and competitive excitement of international trade. The frustrated potters of Europe, unable to reproduce the true porcelain of China, conducted ceaseless "scientific" experiments toward a substitute.

When Marco Polo returned from the court of Kublai Khan in the thirteenth century, he named the rare pieces he brought with him "porcellana," because their glossy surface and texture reminded him of a seashell he knew—a cowrie called in Italian "porcella." The resemblance was indeed marked.

It was natural that the extreme rarity of porcelain made it almost the exclusive monopoly of rulers and princes, who vied with one another to build their collections of both Chinese and Japanese varieties. Kings of France, sultans of Egypt, doges of Venice—all were avid collectors of Chinese porcelain. The intense interest of Augustus the Strong, Elector of Saxony (1670–1733), not only made him Europe's leading collector but eventually led, under his patronage, to the historic discovery in 1708 of true porcelain-making for the first time outside China. Legend has it that Augustus once traded an entire regiment of dragoons for a collection of some forty-eight porcelain vases.

Maria, daughter of Charles Augustus, married in 1743 to King Charles of the Two Sicilies, brought as part of her dowry a large collection of superb Meissen porcelain. This so kindled her husband's interest that he established in Naples his own manufactory, which he later moved to Buen Retiro in Madrid when he became King Carlos III of Spain in 1759.

Madame Pompadour, strongly supporting the royal porcelain factories of Vincennes and Sèvres, joined Louis XV in personally selling the output to members of the French court. Madame is quoted as saying that "Not to buy this china, as long as one has any money, is to prove oneself a bad citizen." The lady apparently believed in the hard sell.

Porcelain was used not only for newly popular beverages such as tea, coffee, and chocolate, but in a wide variety of household objects: basins, bird cages, toilet seats, clock frames, statuettes, snuff boxes, vases, plaques, cane handles, even fireplaces and entire rooms, not to mention the entire range of table services for both personal use and presentation.

The mystery of porcelain's composition gave rise to many beliefs about its magical powers, one being its efficacy in the detection of poison. (It is true that porcelain changes when subjected to caustic alkalis.)

Throughout the eighteenth century, potters and painters of porcelain were bribed or otherwise lured away with their secrets and talents to new lands and new factories. This was indeed industrial espionage.

Eventually, as the process of porcelain manufacture became generally known and perfected, the mystery and the magic faded, giving way to established and commercially profitable enterprises, several of which continue to this day.

Thus, the story of porcelain offers something for everyone: artist, collector, adventurer, trader, scientist, historian, inventor, and businessman. An international saga spanning a dozen centuries, the history of porcelain has involved nearly every aspect of man's endeavor. It is difficult to imagine a subject of more varied and compelling attraction.

Aesthetically, porcelain forms and their decoration reflect the artistic tastes and styles of each succeeding era; i.e., Rococo, Baroque, Louis Seize, Empire, Neoclassical, and so on. Porcelain, in short, was always a sensitive part of its period. As the porcelains of each era were manufactured and then shipped around the world, they became international sources of form and design.

Pair of Ice Pails
Worcester (English), *c.* 1810
Decoration: Aesop Fables painted in colors
(*Courtesy The Detroit Institute of Arts,
Detroit, Michigan.
Gift of Founders Society,
General Endowment Fund*)

14

HARD- AND SOFT-PASTE PORCELAIN

One is first attracted to fine antique porcelain because it is beautiful to look at and pleasant to touch or use. Soon one wishes to know more: How does one make something at once so hard and so fragile, resonant, nonporous, and (usually) translucent, a result so obviously superior—artistically, physically, and chemically—to the lesser products of pottery or earthenware?

For centuries this was a secret known only to the Chinese. If the Chinese perhaps first achieved a true porcelain in the ninth century, they had known how to make a glazed stoneware before that—probably long before the birth of Christ.

True porcelain (called hard paste) has two principal ingredients. The first is kaolin, a white clay composed of aluminum silicate. Because it fires white and withstands extremely high temperatures, kaolin is the basic material of porcelain. The second ingredient is a more fusible feldspathic clay called pentuntse. When prepared—washed, pulverized, and sieved, then mixed with kaolin—pentuntse fuses into a kind of natural glass or glaze. Fired together, kaolin and pentuntse produce true, hard-paste porcelain.

Once the kaolin and pentuntse are combined (pounded and kneaded), the resulting mixture is left to mature. When the potter forms his article, either on a wheel or by using molds, he allows it to dry before firing it at extremely high temperatures (1300–1400° C.). Colored decoration, produced by using metallic oxides such as cobalt, copper, and iron, can be added before firing or afterward; in the latter case, the article is fired again at a lower temperature (900° C.) to set the final glaze.

The entire sequence of porcelain manufacture as practiced by the Chinese can be seen in the charming, contemporary watercolors that were made to illustrate the processes of manufacture for foreign traders. No foreigner was permitted on the scene, inland from Canton. From the first arrival of the clays from nearby mountain deposits, through the preparation of the final mixture, shaping, firing, decorating, and even packing—the whole process is drawn with characteristic Chinese detail.

Long frustrated in their inability to duplicate the Chinese formula for making true porcelain, Europeans turned to other solutions in their efforts to approximate the material they so admired.

In Florence, Italy, toward the end of the sixteenth century, the Medici achieved an artificial porcelain that was translucent and at least resembled the real thing. This formula, however, was lost and not rediscovered until about 1673 in Rouen, France, by Louis Poterat. This led eventually to the artificial, or soft-paste, porcelain manufactories at Saint-Cloud and Chantilly, near Paris.

Artificial, or soft-paste, porcelain (called *pâte tendre* by the French) is basically a white clay mixed with powdered glass. Fired first in the "biscuit," or unglazed, state, it is glazed later at lower temperatures. Thus, the artificial glaze is thicker than that of true porcelain and lies more obviously on the top. True porcelain is feldspathic, formed from the china stone used for the body and fired at the same time.

Because artificial porcelain proved very difficult to work with, suffering excessive breakage and wastage in the kilns, experiments were made, especially in England, to strengthen the body by adding calcined bones or bone ash; soap-rock was also used. Eventually there developed the formula of clays and bone ash that produced the standard English bone china.

Thus the European potters struggled to create a material that in its translucent appearance, at least, was as close as they could come to Chinese hard-paste porcelain.

In Europe the breakthrough came in 1709, when Johann Friedrich Böttger told Augustus the Strong that he could in fact make true, fine, white porcelain. The Royal Saxon Porcelain Manufactory was founded at Meissen, near Dresden, in 1710. By 1713, the Meissen factory was able to produce true porcelain on a commercial scale, with a first offering that year at the Leipzig Fair. Böttger lived until 1719, having established Meissen as the finest porcelain in Europe. Meissen reversed the domination and influence of the Oriental potter and set porcelain standards unrivaled for fifty years.

Despite all efforts to maintain the secret of the Meissen formula, workmen were soon lured from Dresden to Vienna and Venice, usually by the ambassadors of these powers at the Saxon court. The factory in Vienna was established in 1718, that in Venice in 1720, though neither ever really challenged the preeminence of Meissen. Eventually hard-paste porcelain was also made in Vincennes (1740) and Sèvres (1756).

In England, most factories continued the manufacture of artificial, soft-paste porcelain at such places as Bow, Chelsea, Worcester, and Derby. Only at Plymouth, Bristol, and Newhall was true porcelain made in England, and then only briefly.

American collectors are often amazed to learn that possibly the first true porcelain made in the English-speaking world may have been produced in Savannah, Georgia, by a Huguenot potter named Andrew Duché. There are indications that sometime between 1731 and 1738, Duché, apparently in Virginia, found deposits of kaolin, called "unaker" by the Cherokee Indians. In 1743, with help from General Oglethorpe, Duché went to England to market his discovery—his porcelain, or even more likely, the raw materials, which could be shipped as ballast to England. Yet, despite his conversations with such well-known English potters as Frye and Cookworthy, nothing came of Duché's trip and he returned to America. Actually the evidence is slight that Duché ever produced true porcelain, since no surviving examples are known.

The first American porcelain we do know about was produced by two potters named Gousse Bonnin and George Anthony Morris, who established a factory in Philadelphia in December, 1769, using English workmen and clays from nearby Delaware. Bonnin and Morris porcelain is perhaps most like English Bow and Worcester. Authenticated pieces can be found in such museum collections as the Philadelphia Museum of Art, Brooklyn Museum, Smithsonian, Winterthur, and Williamsburg. Financial difficulties brought about the closing of the Philadelphia factory in 1772.

Thus, many centuries after the Chinese discovered the secret of true porcelain manufacture, it became common knowledge. All that had happened in between—the searches, the experimentation, the successes and failures—provide the fascinating story of this fine art.

16

Incense Burner, Ch'ing-pai type
Chinese (Sung), 960–1279
Decoration: Pale blue monochrome
(*Courtesy Center of Asian Art and Culture,*
The Avery Brundage Collection,
San Francisco, California)

CHINESE PORCELAIN

The story, as well as the study, of porcelain begins of course where porcelain itself originated—in China. The evolution from primitive, unglazed pottery to the perfected material took centuries. So vast and complex a subject cannot be usefully summarized in this book, and the new collector is referred to other surveys for a basic understanding of Chinese porcelain in its finest and most important periods. In books and in museums, one may also become familiar with the forms and decoration of Chinese porcelain, particularly as it influenced the tastes and trends of potters all over the world.

A few selected facts and comments may prove helpful here.

The Chinese never revealed the full secret of their method of porcelain manufacture, thus increasing the mystery and the desirability of something the Westerner was not able to duplicate until the eighteenth century.

The Chinese generally preferred the porcelain they made for themselves: its purity and beauty of form, its restraint of decoration, and the superior quality of its body and glaze. They tended to look upon "special order," or "export," porcelain made for foreigners as heavy, coarse, overdecorated, and generally inferior—and it usually was.

True porcelain was probably first achieved during the Sung dynasty (960–1279 A.D.). The Sung Ting ware was of fine quality: a translucent body with a thin, colorless glaze and the decoration, if any, incised or molded.

Chinese blue-and-white porcelain, so influential in the West, saw great excellence in the wares of Hsuan Te, a Ming dynasty reign of 1426–35.

Most familiar to Western collectors were the porcelains of two Ch'ing dynasty reigns: K'ang Hsi (1662–1722) and Ch'ien Lung (1736–95).

Only a very few experts understand and can properly interpret reign marks to date Chinese porcelain. It was a common practice for potters of one reign to compliment an earlier reign with close copies of its porcelain, including the marks.

The Chinese use of elaborate symbolism as decorative devices on porcelain—bats, fish, flowers, birds, animals, and trees to represent longevity, health, happiness, virtue, wealth, and other good things— is worthy of study because the symbols appear regularly on many porcelain objects of both East and West.

Reliable surveys of Chinese porcelain may be found in the following books:

W. B. Honey, *Ceramic Art of the Far East*. London: Faber and Faber, Ltd., 1945.

Anthony du Boulay, *Chinese Porcelain*. New York: G. P. Putnam's Sons, 1953.

George Savage, *Porcelain Through the Ages*. Baltimore: Penguin Books, Pelican Paperbacks, 1963.

White Vase, "Hsing yao" type
Chinese (T'ang), eighth–ninth century
Decoration: Creamy white glaze
(*Courtesy Center of Asian Art and Culture,*
The Avery Brundage Collection,
San Francisco, California)

The principal Chinese dynasties and some of their major contributions to the development of porcelain are:

1122–249 B.C.	CHOU	Glazed pottery
206 B.C.–A.D. 220	HAN	Proto porcelain
618–906	T'ANG	First true, hard-paste, resonant porcelain
960–1279	SUNG	Colored glazes
1280–1368	YÜAN	First blue-and-white porcelain
1368–1644	MING	Decoration in enamel colors
1644–1912	CH'ING	Development of export porcelain trade

1662–1722	K'ANG HSI	Reigns
1723–35	YUNG CHÊNG	of
1736–95	CH'IEN LUNG	Ch'ing
1796–1820	CHIA CH'ING	dynasty
1821–50	TAO KUANG	

1853   Imperial factory at Ching-tê-Chên burned; rebuilt in 1864

1912 on   The Chinese Republic

Note

For other pertinent dates and references, see also the appendixes—Chronology, Glossary, Bibliography, and Public Collections of Antique Porcelain—and the illustrations.

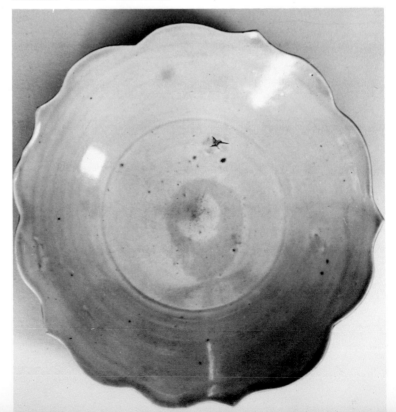

Bowl, Ting
Chinese (Sung), 960–1279
Incised Decoration
(*Courtesy Smithsonian Institution,*
Freer Gallery of Art,
Washington, D. C.)

White Dish
Chinese (T'ang), ninth–tenth century
(*Courtesy The Brooklyn Museum,*
Brooklyn, New York.
Gift of Frederick D. Pratt)

Bowl, Ko Ware
Chinese (Sung), 960–1279
Decoration: Greenish-gray fine crackle with
engraved poem attributed to Chien Lung
(*Courtesy The Detroit Institute of Arts,
Detroit, Michigan.
Gift of Mrs. Richard H. Webber*)

Ming Stem Cup
Chinese (Yüan), 1260–1368
Decoration: Blue and white
(*Courtesy Center of Asian Art and Culture,
The Avery Brundage Collection,
San Francisco, California*)

OPPOSITE, ABOVE: Bowl, Porcelaneous Stoneware, Ting type
Chinese (T'ang), tenth century
Decoration: White and cream glaze;
wide mouth, lobed sides
(*Courtesy Philadelphia Museum of Art,
Philadelphia, Pennsylvania.
The George Crofts Collection: Given by Charles H. Ludington.
Photograph by A. J. Wyatt, staff photographer*)

OPPOSITE, BELOW: Bowl
Chinese (Ming), 1426–1435. Mark of Hsuan Të
Decoration: Underglaze blue
(*Courtesy The Brooklyn Museum,
Brooklyn, New York.
Gift of Helen B. Waterman*)

Bowl, Judgment of Paris (one of many mythological subjects
reproduced on Chinese Export)
Chinese Export, *c.* 1740–1770
Decoration: Polychrome and gilt, fleur-de-lis border
(*Courtesy The Henry Francis du Pont Winterthur Museum,
Winterthur, Delaware*)

PORCELAIN AND THE CHINA TRADE

Trade relations between Europe and the Far East existed as early as
the fourth century B.C. The silk road to Asia and the sea route to India
were established by the first century A.D. Yet Europeans did not see examples of Chinese porcelain until the thirteenth century, when Marco Polo
returned to Venice with several pieces. The more Westerners saw of this
rare and mysterious ware, the greater became their desire to see and own
more and to know more about it—especially the secret of its manufacture.
After 1498, following the opening of Vasco da Gama's new sea route to
India, porcelain reached Europe in greater quantity. The first Portuguese
trading ship landed at Canton in 1517. By 1602, both the English and
the Dutch East Indies companies had been established for trade with the
Orient. Soon after this, the flow of porcelain to Europe became enormous.
Also, in 1602, the first porcelain-laden ship, a Portuguese carrack, was
captured by the Dutch and its cargo of one hundred thousand pieces of
porcelain was auctioned in Holland. The Dutch historian T. Volker esti-
mates that between 1604 and 1657, over 3 million pieces of Oriental
porcelain reached Europe, chiefly through the port of Amsterdam.

The Portuguese and Dutch were followed to Canton by the English,
the French, Swedes, other Europeans, and finally, with Independence, the
Americans. In all, some thirteen Western nations flew their flags over the
trading posts, or "hongs," leased annually in Canton.

Life for the foreign trader at Canton was rigidly prescribed by the emperor's officials. The Westerner was allowed to remain at Canton only for the months of the trading season; he could not move outside his limited compound, a narrow enclave about one-quarter of a mile in length and seven hundred feet wide; he could not bring his wife with him; and he had to conduct all his business through officially appointed hong merchants or agents. Foreign ships were anchored at Whampoa, some twelve miles down the Pearl River from Canton. It must be admitted that the stringent supervision of Western traders had some real cause: the Chinese experience of the savage and arrogant Europeans who first came to the East. The Portuguese and Dutch acted badly not only toward the Chinese (as did the Spanish in Manila) but also toward one another. And the English must be eternally blamed for forcing widespread opium addiction in China with enormous shipments of the drug from India.

The diaries and logs of Western mariners in the China trade make fascinating reading—replete as they are with adventure and hazard on the high seas, difficult relations with the Chinese, life in the exotic East, and the enormous profits that rewarded the successful completion of their long voyage home from Cathay.

The manufacture of porcelain was centered not at Canton, but six hundred miles inland, at Ching-tê-Chên, where the population exceeded 1 million and the smoke of over three thousand kilns could be seen for miles. The finished product reached Canton by a land and river route, just as the porcelain destined for Peking went by barge over the Yangtze River and the Grand Canal. Much porcelain made to foreign order was sent undecorated to Canton, where there was a flourishing business in completing the armorial crests and other designs sent from Europe and America. During the Ming and later periods, porcelain was made by the Chinese at places other than Ching-tê-Chên. For example, from Fukien came the creamy white, richly glossy porcelain called blanc de Chine. The entire process of porcelain manufacture in China was built on production-line principles, each workman, from potter to decorator, being assigned a particular phase of the process. It is said that at Ching-tê-Chên a single piece of porcelain might pass through as many as seventy hands.

Public and private collections today contain examples of Chinese porcelain made to order for a dozen countries. Identification is usually made by a nautical flag, ship, armorial design, or other device. It is this Chinese Export ware that the English and Americans for so many years called Lowestoft, an error first made by William Chaffers, writing in 1863. Chaffers confused Oriental porcelain exported to Europe with a soft-paste porcelain made in the town of Lowestoft, England, in the eighteenth century. There was no connection. At any rate, Chinese Export is the name now generally accepted for the ware that revolutionized the tea-drinking habits of the English, as well as the entire world of the porcelain collector and maker.

In the first half of the nineteenth century, trade at Canton dwindled gradually as European tastes changed. Chinese porcelain production for export was curtailed (Ching-tê-Chên burned in 1853), and Western factories found more efficient, less costly methods of producing both earthenware and porcelain.

Pair of Vases
Chinese (K'ang Hsi), 1662–1722
Decoration: Famille verte
(*Courtesy The Metropolitan Museum of Art,
New York, New York.
The Altman Collection, 1914*)

CHINESE EXPORT PORCELAIN:
A DESIGN CHECKLIST

The enormous flood of Chinese Export porcelain which reached the outside world from the sixteenth to nineteenth centuries reflected not only the changing and widely varying tastes of the countries and periods involved, but also the mark of the myriad Chinese potters and artists who interpreted these orders, often with an engaging ignorance of what they were copying from models, drawings, and other instructions. The following brief checklist represents only those categories of export porcelain most popular in the Western world. The range of variation within each category is extensive.

1. CANTON: Porcelain decorated in underglaze blue; typically a river and temple scene with dark blue lattice border and scalloped edge. Wide variation in quality; earlier wares finely painted, later nineteenth-century pieces poor in color and execution. Named for city from which it was shipped. Same design in apple green enamel is extremely rare.

2. NANKING: Underglaze blue decoration with scenic center. Lattice border finer than Canton; inner border spear-headed rather than scalloped. Later production featured extensive use of overglaze gilt accenting underglaze blue. Named for city on porcelain delivery route.

3. FITZHUGH: Decorated with diapered border with a butterfly or moths and a center wheel or medallion surrounded by four panels bearing Chinese symbols representing music, painting, literature, and philosophy of life. Center medallion often replaced by monogram or other device. Blue and green common Fitzhugh colors, but orange, brown, yellow, mulberry, gold, and black also used. Two colors sometimes appear on one piece. Principally produced 1810–90. Wide variation in quality. Name perhaps derives from a Fitzhugh who headed the Cantonese English East India Company from *c.* 1780 for twelve to fifteen years.

4. ROSE MEDALLION: Wide variety of design but typically decorated with four panels of birds, flowers, and butterflies surrounded by a background of rose tree peonies and green tendrils on gold ground. The later production, common today, extremely inferior to finely executed early decoration.
    NOTE: Rose Medallion (4) and Mandarin (5) are both forms of the earlier Famille Rose pattern.

5. MANDARIN: Typically decorated with panels containing Chinese figures. Borders of flowers, butterflies, birds. Wide variation in design, often much like Rose Medallion or Rose Canton, with extensive use of "famille rose" color. Sometimes orange or sepia monochrome touched with gold.

6. CELADON: A soft, sea green body, usually plain but sometimes decorated with flowers, butterflies in restrained manner. Made for foreign

Tureen, Water Buffalo's Head
Chinese Export, *c.* 1750–1770
Decoration: Painted in tan, blue, gray, lavender, brown
(*Courtesy The Henry Francis du Pont Winterthur Museum, Winterthur, Delaware*)

market from *c.* 1810, with progressively inferior quality. Origins in celadons of earlier Chinese dynasties.

7. CUSTOM DESIGNS: Special orders, family, national, state, organizational devices; monograms, crests, coats of arms, usually arranged in reserve panels, flanked by floral sprigs or other added decoration, borders, and so on. Examples: Masonic Order, Order of the Cincinnati.

8. COPIES: Forms copied from English, French, or other silver, pewter, porcelain, or pottery shapes; i.e., teapots, mugs.

9. MARINE: Ships, national flags, emblems, eagles, battle scenes, custom ordered by mariners in the China trade, ship owners, and so on. Examples exist from a dozen countries.

10. RELIGIOUS: Religious subjects, from prints, were more popular designs in Catholic Europe than America.

11. SPORTING: The English hunt, from contemporary prints, is but one example.

12. BOTANICAL: Various Oriental and Occidental plants and flowers; i.e., tobacco-leaf pattern, frequently combined with birds and butterflies; celery leaves, lotus flowers and leaves, peony, etc.

13. CHINESE SCENES: The hongs, or trading posts, at Canton; treaty ports; river scenes; anchorages such as Whampoa; Chinese figures, mandarins, tea houses, pagodas.

14. CHINESE TASTE: Garniture sets, vases, censers, urns, pagodas in Chinese shapes and taste. Chiefly decorative objects.

15. PRESENTATION: Commemorative pieces marking particular events or occasions; i.e., signing of the American Declaration of Independence.

16. ANIMAL SHAPES: Tureens made in shapes of geese, ducks, fish, water buffalo, wild boar. Also, animal figurines.

17. ARCHITECTURAL: Chinese representations for such buildings as Mount Vernon, the hongs at Canton, the Philadelphia Hospital, and so on.

18. MYTHOLOGICAL: Judgment of Paris, Juno, Jove, often in grisaille or polychrome.

19. AFTER ENGRAVINGS: Cherry Pickers, after Nicholas Lancret, and many others; political, pastoral, religious subjects.

20. HUMAN FIGURES: Both Chinese and Western.

21. BLANC de CHINE: White porcelain made at Te-Hua, Fukien province. Lustrous glaze, beautifully modeled figures. Often decorated in relief, i.e., prunus blossoms. First made in Ming dynasty.

Pieces from Dinner Service
Chinese Export, *c.* 1740–1760
Decoration: Famille rose pattern with sepia gilt
borders, gold-leaf medallions
(*Courtesy The Henry Francis du Pont Winterthur Museum,
Winterthur, Delaware*)

Sample Plate
Chinese Export, *c.* 1785–1810
Decoration: Blue and gilt with four sample borders,
pseudo coat of arms
(*Courtesy The Henry Francis du Pont Winterthur Museum,
Winterthur, Delaware*)

Nanking Mug
Chinese Export, eighteenth century
Decoration: Blue Chinese landscape
(*Courtesy Peabody Museum of Salem,*
Salem, Massachusetts.
Photograph by M. W. Sexton)

Sauce Boat with Tray
Chinese Export, eighteenth century
Decoration: Canton blue and white
(*Courtesy Peabody Museum of Salem,*
Salem, Massachusetts.
Photograph by M. W. Sexton)

Cup and Saucer
Chinese Export, eighteenth century
Decoration: Enamel colors, gilt
(*Courtesy The Metropolitan Museum of Art,*
New York, New York.
Gift of The Winfield Foundation, 1951.
The Helena Woolworth McCann Collection)

Hot Water Tureen with Tray
Chinese Export, eighteenth century
Decoration: Mandarin
(*Courtesy Peabody Museum of Salem,*
Salem, Massachusetts.
Photograph by M. W. Sexton)

Monteith Bowl, footed
Chinese Export, *c.* 1715–1760
Decoration: "Orange peel" surface, coat of arms, blue sprigs
(*Courtesy The Henry Francis du Pont Winterthur Museum,
Winterthur, Delaware*)

"Nanking" Glacier from Dinner Service
Chinese Export, *c.* 1800–1830
Decoration: Blue Chinese landscape, floral borders, gilt band, rim
(*Courtesy The Henry Francis du Pont Winterthur Museum,
Winterthur, Delaware*)

Tea Service (partial)
Chinese Export, *c.* 1750–1770
Decoration: "Cherry Picker" pattern; sepia, floral accents
(*Courtesy The Henry Francis du Pont Winterthur Museum,
Winterthur, Delaware*)

Tureen and Platters from Chadwick Dinner Service
Chinese Export, each piece dated 1791
Decoration: Coat of arms
(*Courtesy Diplomatic Reception Rooms,
U. S. Department of State,
Washington, D.C.,
with the permission of The Dietrich Foundation, Inc.*)

Plate and Bowls
Chinese (Ming), fifteenth century. Hsüan Te Period
Decoration: Blue and white
(*Courtesy Center of Asian Art and Culture,
The Avery Brundage Collection,
San Francisco, California*)

Pieces from Service
Chinese Export, *c.* 1790–1810
Decoration: Marine, with American flag
(*Courtesy The Henry Francis du Pont Winterthur Museum,
Winterthur, Delaware*)

Fruit Basket
Chinese Export, *c.* 1830
Decoration: Green, black, yellow enamel colors.
Oak leaf, acorn borders, sprigs
(*Courtesy Museum of the American China Trade,*
Milton, Massachusetts.
Photograph by George M. Cushing)

Bowl, Cup and Saucer, Teapot
Chelsea (English), eighteenth century
Meissen (German), eighteenth century
Japanese, late seventeenth century
Decoration: Alternating panels of polychrome Chinese
symbols and white spiral motifs on orange-red ground
(*Courtesy National Museum of History and Technology,*
Smithsonian Institution, Washington, D. C.)

Jar, Arita Ware
Japanese, late seventeenth century
Decoration: Blue and white underglaze
(*Courtesy The St. Louis Art Museum,*
St. Louis, Missouri. W. K. Bixby Oriental Art Fund)

JAPANESE PORCELAINS

China was not the only producer of Oriental porcelain. Making a considerably later start was Japanese hard-paste porcelain, which saw its first production about 1616. The clays were Japanese but the knowledge was Chinese and Korean. Between 1640 and 1646, the first Japanese use of polychrome enamel decoration was introduced by a family of potters named Saikaida, the first representative of whom was named Kakiemon (1596–1666). It was this extremely fine and beautiful Kakiemon porcelain, with its delicately restrained decoration, which exerted such a marked influence on Meissen, on French factories like Chantilly, and on such English factories as Chelsea, Bow, and Worcester. Faithfully copied or adapted throughout the ceramic world, with its unmistakable elements: quail, tiger, dragon, phoenix, hedge, plum, pine, etc., Kakiemon was universally admired. Japanese "Imari" designs, on the other hand, were largely bold, ornate, and unrestrained, usually covering the entire surface of the porcelain. Derived from textiles, the Imari decoration featured strong iron-reds, blues, and gold. By the nineteenth century, Imari had reached an ordinary and commercial level.

Japanese porcelains of the seventeenth and eighteenth centuries were largely produced in an area of Hizen Province called Arita, after the principal town in the ceramic center. "Arita" porcelain was also referred to as "Imari" after the port from which most of the production was shipped. The Arita area, in the Saga Prefecture of northern Kyushu, is still today a center of ceramic production. Other early Japanese porcelains of distinctive quality include the production of Nabeshima, Kutani, and Hirado. Although the Japanese themselves generally regard their pottery more highly than their porcelain, early Japanese porcelains are today receiving increased attention from serious collectors.

41

Two plates
(above) Chelsea (English), *c.* 1755
(below) Japanese, *c.* 1700
Decoration: Kakiemon
(*Courtesy National Museum of History and Technology,
Smithsonian Institution, Washington, D. C.*)

Small Plate, Hizen Ware
Japanese, Keian Reign, 1648–1651
Decoration: Pine tree, calligraphy in underglaze blue
(*Courtesy Philadelphia Museum of Art,
Philadelphia, Pennsylvania.
Given by Theodore T. Newbold.
Photograph by A. J. Wyatt, staff photographer*)

Fluted Bowl, Arita Ware
Japanese, Edo Period, late seventeenth century
Decoration: Kakiemon, Shibuemon style
(*Courtesy Seattle Art Museum, Seattle, Washington.*
Eugene Fuller Memorial Collection)

Bowl
Japanese, eighteenth century
Decoration: Eight Dutchmen in underglaze blue panels,
blue inner border
(*Courtesy National Museum of History and Technology,*
Smithsonian Institution, Washington, D.C.)

Bowl, Kutani Ware
Japanese, Early Edo Period, late seventeenth century
Decoration: Polychrome enamels
(*Courtesy The Detroit Institute of Arts,*
Detroit, Michigan. The L. A. Young Fund)

Plate, Kutani Ware
Japanese, second half seventeenth century
Decoration: Polychrome enamels
(*Courtesy The Cleveland Museum of Art,*
Cleveland, Ohio. Gift from various donors by exchange

Standing Figure of a Beauty, Kakiemon Ware
Japanese, Edo Period, c. 1690
Decoration: Polychrome enamels
(*Courtesy The Cleveland Museum of Art,
Cleveland, Ohio. John L. Severance Fund*)

Footed Dish, Nabeshima Ware
Japanese, first half eighteenth century
Decoration: Underglaze blue with overglaze enamel
(*Courtesy Nelson Gallery—Atkins Museum,
Kansas City, Missouri. Nelson Fund*)

THE
IDENTIFICATION
OF
ANTIQUE PORCELAIN

Collecting antique porcelain would be enormously simplified if we could rely on some consistent and unchangeable system of identifying hallmarks. Unfortunately, for many reasons, nothing of this sort exists. Marks could easily be copied, faked, altered, or added at a later date. The Chinese were prone to copy reign marks from earlier porcelains they greatly admired, and European manufacturers copied one another's marks. Only well into the nineteenth century did factories begin to employ systems of established marking—partially to facilitate reorders and to lend the prestige of an old and respected name to new production. In general, it is best to make use of porcelain marks merely as confirming factors in identifications already reached. Excellent books of marks are available (see the bibliography), although no one such book is comprehensive.

Decoration, as already noted, is also a rather unreliable guide to certain identification. Porcelain painters tended to migrate from factory to factory, even from country to country. Outside decorators were often employed, and in slack periods porcelain accumulated—to be decorated later, at or outside the factory. Overglaze decoration was often added at a later date in another factory or country, as, for example, Chinese porcelains decorated in Holland and England. Patterns that became popular or highly valued were widely, and often beautifully, copied throughout the world. This was particularly true of Meissen and Sèvres ware. Finally, certain factories absorbed other factories, including models and molds. They also experimented with various formulas, always seeking a finer, more durable paste.

In this somewhat dismaying absence of reliable guidelines (at least, simple ones), the collector must slowly and patiently build his own expertise.

1. Start by learning the basic differences, visual and otherwise, between true, or hard-paste, porcelain and artificial, or soft-paste, porcelain. This step alone clears up entire areas of identification, since we know who made what paste and who did not. Study examples in accessible collections; then buy from reputable dealers modest examples of hard- and soft-paste pieces for personal handling and study. Supplement this knowledge with reference to established authorities and superior color plates in recommended books.

2. Select one factory for more intensive study, learning the particular characteristics of form, body, and glaze—elements that changed during the life of the factory and have been established or authenticated by experts. You will discover that the production of a single factory is by no means of equal interest, merit, or value. This variation is particularly true in the case of Chinese Export porcelain, which over its extensive history was the product of thousands of different hands and skills.

Chinese mallet
vase, Celadon
Sung Dynasty
(A.D. 960–1279)
*(Courtesy the
Smithsonian Institution,
Freer Gallery of
Art, Washington, D.C.)*

The Kakiemon patterns first introduced in seventeenth century Japanese Arita porcelain were a major influence in the spread of eighteenth-century interest in porcelain. Drawing on China for a knowledge of colored enamels, the Kakiemon potters applied this to porcelain decoration in a uniquely Japanese manner. This featured a restrained use of the available porcelain surface and a charming arrangement of varied elements, including tigers, dragons, birds, flowers, bamboo, pine, and a banded fence, in various combinations. The Kakiemon palette included an orange-red, azure blue, opaque yellow, sea and grass greens, and some gold. The examples of Kakiemon decoration shown here represent only a few of the porcelain factories which either copied or adapted these popular designs. The same decoration may also be found on contemporary eighteenth-century Chinese porcelain, Dutch Delft, and English salt glaze. *(From the author's collection)*

Japanese Kakiemon-style decoration

LEFT: Japanese plate, eighteenth century
Japanese dish, c. 1680
Bow (English) plate, eighteenth century

BELOW: Chelsea—Derby (English) tankard,
eighteenth century
Meissen (German) charger, c. 1735
Chantilly (French) jug, eighteenth century
Worcester (English) tankard, eighteenth century,
Dr. Wall period

Chinese fish jar, Wu-Ts'ai type
Ching Dynasty (c. A.D. 1522–1566)
(Courtesy the Avery Brundage Collection,
M. H. de Young Memorial Museum,
San Francisco, California)

Japanese Imari-style decoration
Vienna, Du Paquier period,
two small dishes, tureen
Meissen (German) large dish, c. 1731
(Courtesy the Delhom Collection,
Mint Museum of Art,
Charlotte, North Carolina)

Meissen (German) eighteenth century
Chocolate pot
Gold chinoiserie decoration
*(Courtesy the Delhom Collection,
Mint Museum of Art,
Charlotte, North Carolina)*

Meissen (German), c. 1724
Pair of chocolate cups, saucers
Decorated by Johann C. Höroldt
*(Courtesy Cummer Gallery of Art,
Jacksonville, Florida)*

Vincennes (French), c. 1750
Soup dish with stand
*(Courtesy the Campbell Museum
Collection, Camden, New Jersey)*

3. Rely on reputable dealers to expand and develop your firsthand knowledge of antique porcelain. The best dealers are prepared to be helpful and from their stock or private collections can show you examples of almost every factory.

4. Whenever possible, in this country and abroad, visit the great museum collections of porcelain. You cannot, of course, handle the pieces, but you can learn much from simple comparative observations of the finest surviving porcelains, in terms of form, decoration, and authenticated dating of manufacture.

Chemistry provides yet another area of identification, which in the hands of modern experts has added greatly to our knowledge of antique porcelain. The chemical analysis of porcelain—from intact, repaired, or broken examples—tells much. For example, the presence of a large percentage of phosphoric acid indicates that bone ash was a principal ingredient in the formula, as in Bow porcelain; magnesium oxide suggests a soapstone formula, and so on. For the student with a scientific bent, George Savage has written an excellent chapter on the chemical analysis of porcelain in his book *18th Century English Porcelain.*

In the same chapter, Mr. Savage also explains for the layman the application of physics to the process of identification, particularly the use of light—transmitted, reflected, and ultraviolet—as an aid to attribution. Certainly every collector can use ultraviolet light to advantage in the detection of repairs and other types of restoration. Repairs and added decorations show up sharply under this light. Short-wave light works effectively for identification; long wave is good for spotting repairs (see the bibliography for where to obtain some of these devices). As a matter of habit, always ask the dealer if repairs have been made. Do not hesitate to buy repaired porcelain when a piece is of special interest or rarity and when repairs have been skillfully executed. And be sure the invoice of each item purchased is specifically descriptive with regard to factory, age, and condition.

Copies, Reproductions, and Fakes

If a piece of antique porcelain is not wholly geniune, original, and intact—yet at first looks so to the naked eye—one of four things has probably happened: (1) A corner, a handle, a head, a hand, or some other piece has been broken off and put back. Well done, there is no harm in this as long as you know what you have and what you are buying. Ultraviolet light is most helpful here. (2) The original piece has been deliberately tampered with by the removal of some decoration and the application of different, rarer, or additional decoration. (3) The piece is wholly false and a copy of an earlier, or even a contemporary but more distinguished, manufacture. (4) The piece bears the added mark of a famous factory—its own mark, if any, having perhaps been removed. Remember that many early potters had no idea their work would someday be collected and identification become important. To them, marks were incidental.

All copies and reproductions were not, or are not, intended to deceive and defraud. We know that the Chinese and Europeans copied earlier porcelains (with or without original marks) that they greatly admired.

Factories such as Samson and Vivinis in Paris made porcelain copies as replacements for broken services and employed clearly individual and published marks of their own. Today we have a whole range of copies, especially of such currently popular porcelain as Chinese Export. These copies are no more than what they pretend to be—anywhere from atrocious to acceptable modern reproductions that can be both useful and decorative.

There have always been greedy, unscrupulous dealers who will knowingly offer a piece of porcelain as antique, mint, and original, when it is not. Beware of the obvious, the historically rare piece offered as a bargain; avoid the large collections of Chinese Export proffered in the Far East—an unlikely source. Stay with the reputable dealers who are willing to give you a fully detailed descriptive invoice, including factory name and approximate year of manufacture.

It is not as difficult as it might seem to train the mind and the eye to spot the spurious. You will find the production of a soft-paste factory (most of the English ones) copied in hard paste. You will see that the copyist could not resist adding that extra decoration, the extra American eagle, and thus the restraint of the original, as well as its charm, has been lost. Be informed, be aware, and be cautious. You will make mistakes, as we all do, but you can surely arm yourself against major disasters and disappointments.

Finally, there is a growing body of knowledge on the subject of fakes and forgeries, together with an increasingly effective use of technical examination. Read what the experts have to say and benefit accordingly.

"Lovers with a Birdcage," or "Crinoline Group"
J. J. Kaendler, modeler
Meissen (German), c. 1736–1740
Decoration: Enamel colors and gilt on white porcelain
(Courtesy The Metropolitan Museum of Art,
New York, New York. Gift of Alex and Richard Ball, 1942)

EIGHTEENTH-CENTURY GERMAN PORCELAIN

AFTER CENTURIES OF FRUITLESS EFFORT TO REPRODUCE THE
TRUE PORCELAIN OF THE ORIENT, SUCCESS CAME AT MEISSEN,
NEAR DRESDEN, SAXONY, IN 1708. FROM THIS HISTORIC DE-
VELOPMENT CAME THE SUPERB PORCELAINS OF MEISSEN.
INITIAL ORIENTAL DECORATIVE INFLUENCE GRADUALLY GAVE
WAY TO EUROPEAN THEMES. THE GREAT NAMES AT MEISSEN
INCLUDE THOSE OF JOHANN BOTTGER, FOUNDER-DISCOVERER;
JOHANN HEROLD, GIFTED PAINTER; AND J. J. KAENDLER,
MASTER MODELER OF FIGURE GROUPS. MEISSEN'S HIGH QUALITY
OF DESIGN, DECORATION, AND EXECUTION PROVIDED EX-
AMPLES AND STANDARDS FOR ALL WHO FOLLOWED, INCLUD-
ING NUMEROUS OTHER GERMAN FACTORIES.

Monkey with Snuff Box
Meissen (German), *c.* 1730
Decoration: Black, with gold box; lavender, green base
(*Courtesy Museum of Fine Arts, Boston, Massachusetts.*
William Francis Warden Fund)

Two figures: Gardener and Companion
Höchst (German), *c.* 1750
Decoration: Costumes in black, white, salmon;
green, yellow, brown accents
(*Courtesy The Metropolitan Museum of Art,
New York, New York. Gift of R. Thornton Wilson, 1950,
in memory of Florence Ellsworth Wilson*)

Teapot
Meissen (German), *c.* 1718
Decoration: Gold chinoiserie
(*Courtesy Cummer Gallery of Art,
Jacksonville, Florida*)

Squirrels
J. J. Kaendler, modeler
Meissen (German), *c.* 1732
Decoration: White with brown, black markings, applied flowers.
Ormolu mounts, *c.* 1740
(*Courtesy The Metropolitan Museum of Art, New York, New York.*
Gift of R. Thornton Wilson, 1950, in memory of Caroline Astor Wilson)

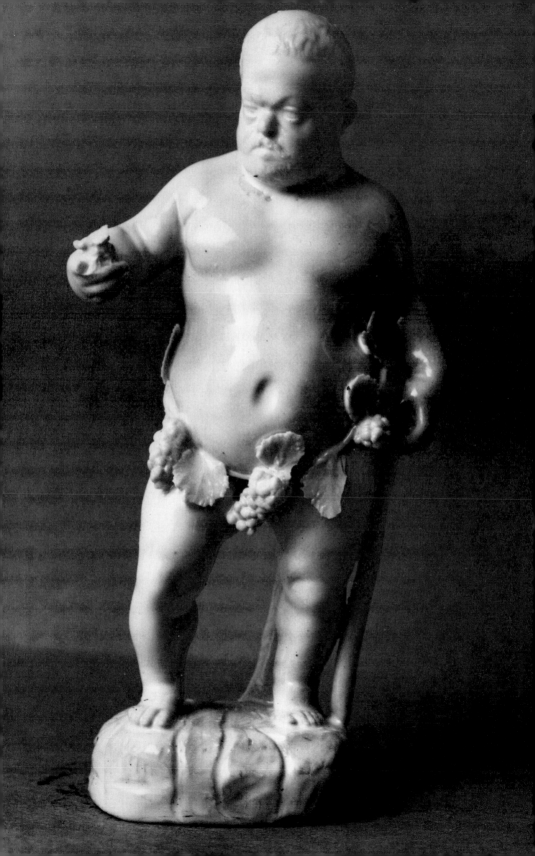

EIGHTEENTH-CENTURY CONTINENTAL PORCELAINS

DESPITE EFFORTS AT MEISSEN TO GUARD ITS SECRET OF TRUE
PORCELAIN'S COMPOSITION AND MANUFACTURE, MEISSEN
WORKMEN WERE SOON LURED AWAY TO VIENNA, VENICE, AND
OTHER CITIES IN EUROPE. BEFORE THE CLOSE OF THE EIGH-
TEENTH CENTURY, FACTORIES ON THE CONTINENT WERE
IMITATING THE SUPERB PORCELAINS OF MEISSEN, OR, LATER,
SÈVRES—YET SELDOM ACHIEVING THE SAME QUALITY OR
SUCCESS.

White Figure, Morgante the Dwarf
Doccia Factory (Italian), *c.* 1750–1755
(*Courtesy Delhom Collection, The Mint
Museum of Art, Charlotte, North Carolina*)

Teapot
Capodimonte (Italian), 1760
Decoration: Italian ruins on
yellow, gilt background
(*Courtesy The Metropolitan
Museum of Art, New York, New York.
Rogers Fund, 1906*)

Dish, The Death of King Saul
Medici (Italian), *c.* 1580–1600
Decoration: Underglaze blue
with medallions, flowers
(*Courtesy The Metropolitan Museum
of Art, New York, New York.
The Samuel D. Lee Fund, 1941*)

Chinese Figure
Vezzi (Italian), *c.* 1723
Venice
Decoration: Polychrome—red, yellow, blue, green
(*Courtesy The Metropolitan Museum of Art,
New York, New York. Gift of
R. Thornton Wilson, 1950, in
memory of Florence Ellsworth Wilson*)

Teapot
Vienna, Du Paquier Period, *c.* 1730–1740
Decoration: Floral (Indianische Blumen) copied from Meissen
(*Courtesy National Museum of History and Technology,
Smithsonian Institution, Washington, D. C.*)

Plate
Tournai (Belgium), *c.* 1750–1760
Decoration: Oriental landscapes
and figures in colored enamels
(*Courtesy The Metropolitan
Museum of Art, New York, New York.
Gift of R. Thornton Wilson, 1950,
in memory of Florence Ellsworth Wilson*)

73

Three Figures: Goose vender, peasant
woman holding hen and eggs, and
young man with goat
Copenhagen, *c.* 1780
Decoration: Polychrome with underglaze blue
(*Courtesy National Museum of History and
Technology, Smithsonian Institution, Washington, D. C.*)

One of a Pair of Jars with Silver Gilt Mounts
Chantilly (French), *c.* 1730
Decoration: Biscuit with relief flowers
(*Courtesy Delhom Collection,*
The Mint Museum of Art,
Charlotte, North Carolina)

EIGHTEENTH-CENTURY FRENCH PORCELAIN

THE FINE ARTIFICIAL, OR SOFT-PASTE, PORCELAINS PRODUCED
IN EIGHTEENTH-CENTURY FRANCE WERE INDEBTED TO BOTH
THE MEDICI PORCELAINS OF SIXTEENTH-CENTURY ITALY AND
THOSE MADE IN SEVENTEENTH-CENTURY ROUEN. STRONG
JAPANESE DECORATIVE INFLUENCES CAME FROM THE
PRINCELY COLLECTIONS OF THE ERA. SAINT-CLOUD, CHAN-
TILLY, MENNECY, VINCENNES, AND SÈVRES—EACH WAS DIF-
FERENT, YET ALL SHARED THE SPECIAL WARMTH AND CHARM
SO CHARACTERISTIC OF EIGHTEENTH-CENTURY FRENCH POR-
CELAIN.

Pair of Incense Urns
Mennecy (French), *c.* 1740
Decoration: White animal
groups, relief flowers
(*Courtesy Museum of Fine Arts,*
Boston, Massachusetts.
Bequest of Forsyth Wickes)

Oval Dish
Chantilly (French), *c.* 1750
Decoration: Hunting scene framed
by flowers, gilt work
(*Courtesy Museum of Fine Arts,*
Boston, Massachusetts. Bequest of Forsyth Wickes)

White Figurines
Saint-Cloud (French), Louis XV Period, 1724–1766
(Courtesy Philadelphia Museum of Art,
Philadelphia, Pennsylvania. Given by Mrs. Morris Hawkes.
Photograph by A. J. Wyatt, staff photographer)

Figures, "Le Fluteur," or "The Music Lesson"
Modeled by Fernex after Boucher
Sèvres (French), third quarter eighteenth century
Decoration: Biscuit figure group with sheep, dog, flowers
(Courtesy The Detroit Institute of Arts,
Detroit, Michigan. Founders Society Purchase,
Joseph Boyer Memorial Fund)

Cup and Saucer
Sèvres (French), 1758–1759
Decoration: White blossoms
in relief with blue painted flowers
(*Courtesy The Walters Art Gallery,
Baltimore, Maryland*)

Chocolate Cup with Cover and Saucer
Vincennes (French), *c.* 1753
Decoration: Yellow ground with *putti* and trophies
in monochrome blue on reserved white panels
(*Courtesy The Walters Art Gallery,
Baltimore, Maryland*)

EIGHTEENTH-CENTURY ENGLISH PORCELAIN

ENGLISH PORCELAIN MANUFACTURE, LARGELY SOFT PASTE, DATES FROM ABOUT 1744. UNLIKE THEIR CONTINENTAL COUNTERPARTS, SUPPORTED BY ROYALTY, ENGLISH PORCELAIN FACTORIES WERE COMMERCIAL VENTURES, OFTEN SHORT-LIVED. INFLUENCES ON ENGLISH PORCELAIN WERE BOTH ORIENTAL AND CONTINENTAL. TRUE PORCELAIN WAS MADE BRIEFLY AT BRISTOL, PLYMOUTH, AND NEWHALL. BESIDES THE FINE PRODUCTION OF SUCH FACTORIES AS CHELSEA, BOW, DERBY, AND WORCESTER, ENGLAND'S CHIEF CONTRIBUTIONS TO PORCELAIN MANUFACTURE INCLUDED THE DEVELOPMENT OF A PROCESS FOR TRANSFER PRINTING OF DECORATIVE DESIGNS FROM COPPER PLATES AND THE GRADUAL EVOLUTION OF A STRONGER, MORE DURABLE BODY, USING THE CRUSHED BONES OF ANIMALS—HENCE "BONE CHINA."

Mug, Parrot with Grapes
Worcester (English), Hancock signature, 1765–1770
Black Transfer Print
(*From the author's collection.*
Photograph by Robert Hunt Whitten Assoc.)

Leaf Dish
Longton Hall (English), *c.* 1753–1758
Decoration: Sycamore leaves with
lime-green borders, purple veining
(*Courtesy The Colonial Williamsburg Collection.*
Williamsburg, Virginia)

Mug, King of Prussia
Worcester (English), Hancock signature dated 1757
Black Transfer Print
(*From the author's collection.*
Photograph by Robert Hunt Whitten Assoc.)

Dish
Bow (English), *c.* 1760
Decoration: Oriental figures, landscape on underglaze blue
(*Courtesy Philadelphia Museum of Art,*
Philadelphia, Pennsylvania. Given by Mrs. E. Hollingsworth Siter.
Photograph by A. J. Wyatt, staff photographer)

Standing figures with fruit, "Les Vendangeurs"
Derby (English), 1750–1755
(*Courtesy The Colonial Williamsburg Collection,*
Williamsburg, Virginia)

Teapot
Newhall (English), *c.* 1790
Decoration: Floral design in
crimson, lilac, green, black on white
(*Courtesy Philadelphia Museum of Art,
Philadelphia, Pennsylvania.
Given by Emma Rebecca Pierce.
Photograph by A. J. Wyatt, staff photographer*)

Mug
Lowestoft (English), *c.* 1789
Decoration: Floral sprigs with
printed inscription, "A Trifle from Lowestoft."
Puce, red, green at rim
(*Courtesy The Henry Francis du Pont Winterthur Museum,
Winterthur, Delaware*)

Sauce Boat
Bristol (English), *c.* 1770–1781
Decoration: garlands and acanthus
leaves in green on white background
(*Courtesy The Walters Art Gallery,
Baltimore, Maryland*)

Plate
Chelsea (English), 1753–1758
Decoration: Kakiemon "wheat sheaf" pattern
(*Courtesy The Colonial Williamsburg Collection,
Williamsburg, Virginia*)

Two Figures, Young Woman with Egg
Basket and Young Man with Lamb
and Fruit Basket
Derby (English), eighteenth century
Painted in natural colors
(*Courtesy The Walters Art Gallery,
Baltimore, Maryland*)

Teapot
Plymouth (English), *c.* 1770
Decoration: Oriental—red, blue,
green puce enamel, gold detail;
red, green diaper border
*(Courtesy The Metropolitan Museum of Art,
New York, New York.
Gift of Rev. Alfred Duane Pell, 1902)*

Plate and Mugs
Worcester (English), Dr. Wall Period, 1756–1783
Decoration: Blue scale ground, birds, insects
(*From the author's collection.*
Photograph by Robert Hunt Whitten Assoc.)

EARLY NINETEENTH-CENTURY PORCELAIN

THE ADVENT OF THE NINETEENTH CENTURY FOUND THE
MANUFACTURE OF PORCELAIN ORGANIZED LARGELY ON A
COMMERCIAL BASIS. THE NEW BONE-ASH COMPOSITION PRO-
DUCED A MORE DURABLE BODY. THE DEMAND WAS FOR SHOWY
OPULENCE AND LAVISH DECORATION. IN BOTH THE ORIENT
AND EUROPE THE QUALITY OF PORCELAIN GENERALLY DE-
TERIORATED. WITH SOME NOTABLE EXCEPTIONS, PORCELAINS
WERE ARTISTICALLY UNORIGINAL AND UNINSPIRED. THUS,
AFTER TEN CENTURIES, THE SECRETS OF PORCELAIN—ITS
COMPOSITION AND ITS MANUFACTURE—WERE NOW COMMON
KNOWLEDGE. AN ART HAD BECOME A BUSINESS, AND THE
GREATEST DAYS WERE OVER.

Urn, View of Merchants' Exchange, New York City
Paris, France, c. 1825
Decoration: Polychrome overglaze
colors, gilt detail
(*Courtesy The Metropolitan Museum of Art,
New York, New York.
The Harris Brisbane Dick Fund, 1938*)

Tea Set
Josiah Spode II, Maker
Stoke-on-Trent (English), *c.* 1800–1830
Decoration: Floral in polychrome and gold
(*Courtesy The Metropolitan Museum of Art,
New York, New York. Gift of
Henry G. Marquand, 1894*)

Cup
Derby (English), *c.* 1825 (Bloor)
Decoration: Gilt bands, festoons,
dots, polychrome flowers
(*Courtesy The Brooklyn Museum,
Brooklyn, New York. Gift of Rev.
Alfred Duane Pell*)

Cup and Saucer
Thomas Minton & Sons (English), *c.* 1830
Decoration: Gilt bands, sea shells,
and seaweed in maroon
(*Courtesy The Brooklyn Museum,
Brooklyn, New York. Gift of
Rev. Alfred Duane Pell*)

Pair of Vases, Presidential
Portraits (Adams and Jefferson)
Sèvres (French), nineteenth century
Gilt Decoration
(*Courtesy The Brooklyn Museum,*
Brooklyn, New York)

Pot, Bowl, Cup, and Saucer
Bohemia (German), *c.* 1820–1830
Decoration: White porcelain painted
in colors and gold with human figures
(*Courtesy The Walters Art Gallery,
Baltimore, Maryland. Gift of
Nelson and Juanita Greif Gutman*)

Covered Flagon, Declaration of Independence Scene
Chinese Export, *c.* 1825–1850
Decoration: Spread eagle with orange-red, blue accents
(*Courtesy The Henry Francis du Pont Winterthur Museum,
Winterthur, Delaware*)

AMERICAN PORCELAIN

AMERICA'S FIRST RECORDED PORCELAIN FACTORY WAS ESTAB-
LISHED IN 1769 IN PHILADELPHIA BY BONNIN AND MORRIS,
WITH WORKMEN FROM ENGLAND AND CLAYS FROM NEARBY
DELAWARE. FINANCIAL DIFFICULTIES BROUGHT THE VENTURE
TO AN END IN 1772. ONLY A FEW PIECES SURVIVE. A SECOND
PHILADELPHIA PORCELAIN FACTORY WAS FOUNDED IN 1826
BY WILLIAM TUCKER. TUCKER PORCELAIN HAD A STRONG,
WELL-FIRED BODY CLOSE TO THAT OF BONE-CHINA COMPOSI-
TION. DECORATION WAS CLASSICAL, FOLLOWING CONTEM-
PORARY PRODUCTION IN PARIS FACTORIES. THE TUCKER FIRM
CEASED PRODUCTION IN 1838.

Pitcher
Smith, Fife & Company (American), 1830
Decoration: Painted flowers, gold banding,
gold initials "T. Mc A."
(*Courtesy The Brooklyn Museum, Brooklyn,
New York. Dick S. Ramsay Fund*)

Sauce Boat
Bonnin & Morris
(American), *c.* 1771–1772
Decoration: Blue
and white
(*Courtesy The Brooklyn Museum,
Brooklyn, New York.
Dick S. Ramsay Fund*)

Fruit Bowl
Tucker & Hemphill
(American), *c.* 1832
Decoration: Open-
work in white
(*Courtesy The Brooklyn Museum,
Brooklyn, New York.
Lent by The Philadelphia
Museum of Art*)

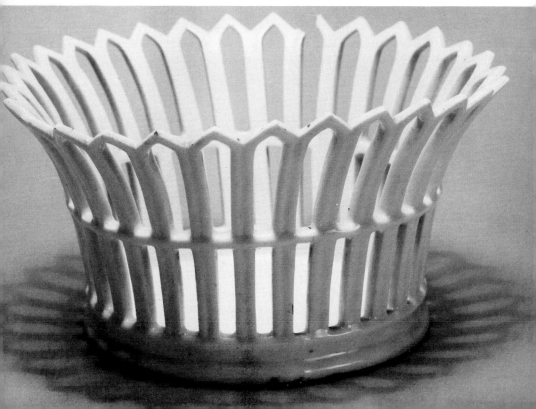

Fruit Dish
John Vickers (American), 1824
Decoration: Painted still
life on white. Dated 1824
(*Courtesy The Henry Francis
du Pont Winterthur Museum,
Winterthur, Delaware*)

Basket with Cover
Bonnin & Morris
(American), *c.* 1770–1772
Decoration: Blue and white
(*Courtesy The Colonial
Williamsburg Collection,
Williamsburg, Virginia*)

Miniature Tea Set
Tucker & Hulme (American), *c.* 1828
Decoration: Gold on white
(*Courtesy Philadelphia Museum of Art,*
Philadelphia, Pennsylvania. Given
by Mrs. Edward S. Sayres.
Photograph by A. J. Wyatt, staff photographer)

Vase, View of
Tucker & Hemphill Factory
Tucker & Hemphill
(American), *c.* 1832–1835
Decoration: Paris style,
with gilt handles
(*Courtesy Philadelphia*
Museum of Art, Philadelphia, Pennsylvania.
Given by Aliza Amanda Tucker
in memory of Thomas Tucker)

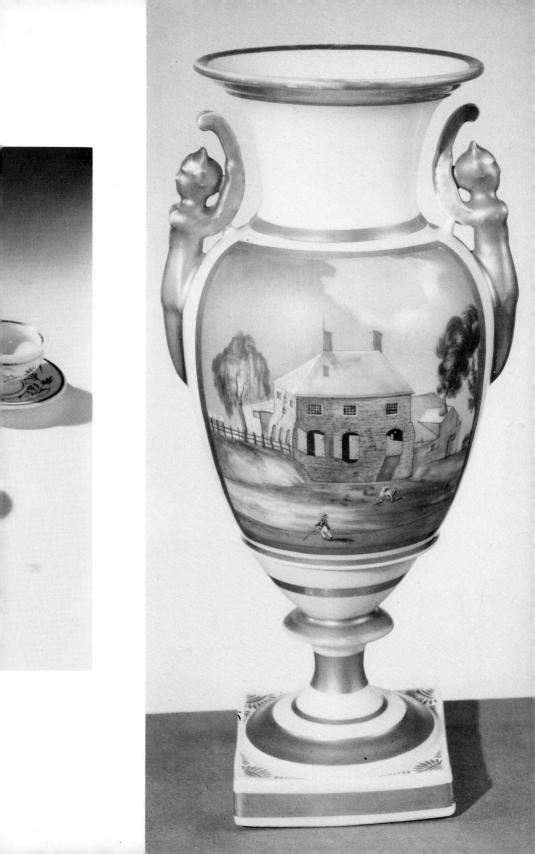

THE DECORATION OF PORCELAIN

What first attracts one to porcelain is, of course, its appearance. Appearance means material, form, proportion, and decoration. Of these, decoration offers perhaps the most interesting range of choices.

The Chinese, in their early period, attached little emphasis to decoration, taking far more interest in form, graceful proportion, and texture. The superb porcelains of the T'ang, Sung, and Ming dynasties are most impressive because of their graceful forms and the pleasing suitability of their monochrome decoration.

Decoration was perhaps more to the Western than to the Chinese taste, and the demand for it developed with the increased manufacture of export porcelain to please foreign buyers who came to China in the seventeenth and eighteenth centuries.

Favorite subjects in the decoration of Chinese porcelain for the West included Oriental scenes; willows, boats, and bridges; armorial crests; floral designs and exotic birds; marine, sporting, and religious representations; historical and mythological figures; scenes taken from popular engravings; and combinations of these. The decoration of European porcelain tended to follow that of the Chinese and Japanese. Many collectors with special interests in these fields often concentrate on a particular decorative style or subject, just as other collectors specialize in particular forms or factories.

Influences on porcelain decoration were as varied as they were complex. Often decorative designs were taken from established silver shapes, as was the shape itself of much porcelain. Some popular decoration was frequently copied by other factories throughout the world. For example, the blue, red, and gold brocadelike pattern of Japanese Imari was extensively copied not only by Europeans but also by the Chinese, from European models taken from the Japanese. The more reserved decoration of Japanese Kakiemon was particularly popular at Meissen and in such French factories as Chantilly, Mennecy, and Saint-Cloud. The early blue-and-white ware that came to Europe from China influenced all design, especially the Dutch, German, and English production of tin-glazed earthenware, such as Delft and Staffordshire.

Naturally, much porcelain reflects the interests of the traveler and trader. Missionaries contributed the Jesuit and other religious designs. Mariners liked the nautical touch. Families ordered porcelain services bearing their coats of arms. Almost every human activity and interest found its way onto the surface of early porcelain.

From an early era in Chinese porcelain, a wide selection of colors was available, alone or in combination. Some colors, such as red and blue, were applied before the first firing. Others were applied after the first firing and then fired again at lower temperatures.

For practical reasons, much Chinese (and later, English) porcelain was decorated at points nearer the market, not at the factory. In China, much porcelain produced inland at Ching-tê-Chên was completed with overglaze decoration at Canton, close to the foreign trader. Chinese porcelain was often shipped to Europe in white, to be decorated there with enamel colors over the glaze. When the European artist added such decoration—either gilding or bright colors such as the Dutch red, green, and yellow—to a piece already decorated, it was known as "clobbering." In such instances, the result was often an overdecorated piece in bad taste.

Identifying porcelain by its decoration is often, but not always, reliable. For example, flower painters in England were inclined to be itinerant, their work appearing on the porcelain of several factories.

England's principal contribution to porcelain decoration came in the application of the transfer print, the relatively simple process of transferring from an engraving, in wet ink, a wet paper print to the white porcelain surface. This method was invented by John Brooks, an Irish engineer. The transfer print, either in black or in color, was a relatively easy and inexpensive process compared to the time-consuming effort of hand decoration.

In general, the decoration of porcelain has followed contemporary tastes and has catered to the people for whom it was done. Frequently, the more prolific the decoration, the later the period.

Any list of superb porcelain decoration must include the Kakiemon of Japan; its copies in Germany, France, and England; the beautifully painted chinoiseries and harbor scenes of Meissen ware; the figures of Meissen and Chelsea; the production of early Worcester and the best of Chinese Export.

The range of porcelain decoration includes the following principal techniques and variations:

1. Underglaze painting
2. Overglaze painting, i.e., with enamels
3. Combinations of 1 and 2, above.
4. Incised and sgraffito
5. Applied, i.e., prunus pattern
6. Pierced
7. Transfer printed
8. Slip (liquid clay)
9. Added decoration: at another time and place, as "clobbered"
10. Porcelain manufactured at one place, decorated at another, i.e., Chinese white porcelain decorated in Holland or England

MAJOR PORCELAIN FACTORIES

BERLIN: Hard-paste porcelain produced 1752–57 by Wilhelm Kaspar Wegely, backed by Frederick the Great. Hard, white paste. Useful and decorative wares after Meissen, relief borders. *Marks: The letter "W" in underglaze blue or impressed with combination of numbers.* In 1763, Frederick the Great purchased the factory established 1761 by Johann Gotzkowsky. Always state owned, factory is known today as Staatliche Porzellanmanufaktur. Eighteenth-century production reached three thousand pieces daily. Hard paste first grayish, later cold white. Wide range of shapes and decoration, frequently inspired by Meissen. Tableware, presentation services. Fine flower painting; relief and pierced decoration. Military, mythological, pastoral, classical subjects. *Marks: Scepter mark 1763–1837. Letters "K.P.M." with orb in red or blue after 1830. Prussian eagle with "K.P.M." 1840–70.*

BONNIN AND MORRIS: First American soft-paste factory, established 1769 in Southwark, Philadelphia, by Gousse Bonnin and George Morris with English workmen and clays from nearby Delaware. First advertisement January 10, 1771. Production of useful and decorative wares most like Worcester and Bow. Financial difficulties resulted in eventual failure 1772. Examples in Philadelphia, Brooklyn, Metropolitan, Smithsonian, Winterthur, and Williamsburg museums. *Marks: Infrequent, as letter "P" in underglaze blue.*

BOW: Founded in Stratford-le-Bow, East London (*c.* 1744–76), by Thomas Frye and Edward Heylin. First wares of heavy body; soft, creamy paste; a waxy, uneven glaze; and not very translucent. Relatively high bone-ash content. Early mellow glaze later became harder, more brilliant. Considerable useful ware in underglaze blue and white. Followed silver shapes and Oriental forms, including decoration after Japanese Kakiemon and Imari; Chinese blanc de Chine. Figures after Meissen models. Some fine flower painting after Chantilly, Mennecy. Excellent transfer printing in colors. *Marks: Complicated; "New Canton" early, or various factory and workmen's marks to 1760, when anchor and dagger in red or underglaze blue were first used.*

BRISTOL: (Lunds) Soft-paste porcelain made in Gloucestershire, England, *c.* 1749–52, by William Miller and Benjamin Lund. Few surviving pieces, i.e., Chinese-type figures—*marked "Bristoll."* Factory absorbed 1752 by Worcester.

BRISTOL: Founded in Gloucestershire, England, by William Cookworthy, who moved his factory from Plymouth in 1770. Richard Champion assumed control in 1772. Patent later acquired by group of New Hall potters. A hard-paste porcelain of high translucency and grayish to clear glaze. Figures based on Derby and Chelsea-Derby. Useful wares decorated with floral sprays and Neoclassical designs. A range from simple cottage ware to elaborate custom services. Figures, vases, teapots. Typical colors a leaf green and a clear, deep red. Sèvres an influence in style, decoration. Bristol rare; made largely for presentation. *Mark: "X," alone or with crossed swords, in blue enamel.*

BUEN RETIRO: Factory transferred in 1759 from Capodimonte, Naples, by King Charles IV Sicily when he became Carlos III of Spain. Large staff of Italian workmen, modelers, painters came to Madrid factory. Soft-paste porcelain like Capodimonte produced until 1804, when hard-paste porcelain was made to closing in 1808. Successive stylistic influences were Rococo, Louis Seize, Neoclassic. Excellent quality figures and decorations. *Marks: Bourbon fleur-de-lis in various forms.*

CAPODIMONTE: Established 1743 near Naples by Charles IV of Sicily. (He later, 1759, moved entire factory, workmen, even considerable clay to Spain when he became Carlos III. Here porcelain was called Buen Retiro.) Fine, soft, creamy paste and translucent body. Figures, vases, tea table services in Baroque style. Painting rivals best of Meissen, Sèvres— after Watteau, Boucher, and Dutch floral painters. Relief decoration characteristic. Doccia factory acquired molds and made Capodimonte fakes, complete with marks, as did German factories. *Mark: Bourbon fleur-de-lis.*

CAUGHLEY: Established 1772 in Broseley, Shropshire, England, by Thomas Turner. John Rose purchased factory 1799. Factory closed 1814. Generally followed Worcester in soapstone body, production of useful wares in blue and white (Caughley blue had violet tone). Robert Hancock, transfer expert, came to Caughley in 1774. *Marks: Imitated those at Worcester; crescent, plus an "S" or "C" in blue, or word "Salopian."* Production resembled Worcester but with a more orange tint to body. Shape, decoration similar.

CHANTILLY: Established 1725 by Louis, Prince de Conde, near Paris. Closed *c.* 1800. Soft paste. Smooth, soft, brilliant glaze, white at first, later a creamy yellow. Meissen and Japanese influence, especially Kakiemon (forms after silver and Oriental shapes). Tableware, tureens, flower pots, toilet pomade pots, handles, and so on. Decoration included red dragon pattern, flower sprigs. Chantilly colors remarkably soft, brilliant. *Marks: Hunting horn in red enamel glaze (1725–60), in blue enamel (1760 on), or incised. Blue mark, with "Chantilly," is late eighteenth century.*

CHELSEA: Four periods: Triangle, 1745–49 (*Mark: Incised triangle*); Raised Anchor, 1750–53; Red Anchor, 1753–58 (Meissen and Chinese, Japanese influences); Gold Anchor, 1758–70 (bone-ash body, Sèvres influence). William Duesbury of Derby purchased factory 1770; Chelsea-Derby period, 1770 to closing in 1784. Paste ranges from early, warm creamy body with "moons," fairly translucent, to increasingly harder texture with bone ash added. Wide variety of production included figure groups, animals and vegetables in tureens, miniature pieces called toys, copies of silver shapes. *Marks: Many pieces unmarked, as above, except Chelsea-Derby marked with Derby "D" over anchor.* Best of Chelsea ranks as England's finest porcelain.

COALPORT: Established 1796 in Coalbrookdale, Shropshire, England, by John Rose, who purchased Caughley, 1799; Swansea, 1820; and Nantgarw, 1822. Early Coalport indistinguishable from Caughley—as decorated at Coalport, 1820–50; excellent flower painting with modeled and applied decoration. Skillful imitation and faking of Sèvres, Meissen, Chelsea models. (White, translucent body.) *Marks: "Coalport"; "Coalbrookdale"; "CD"; "C Dale"; "English Porcelain, Coalport"; "John Rose and Co."* Factory moved to Staffordshire 1926. Coalport China now made at Crescent Works, Stoke-on-Trent, by Coalport China, Ltd.

COPENHAGEN: Founded in Copenhagen, Denmark, 1755, by staff headed by Frantz Henrich Muller. Louis Fournier joined factory 1759, from France. Purchased by state in 1779. Subsequent development under various managements, becoming private concern 1867; continues today. Early bluish-gray hard paste became whiter, more translucent by 1780. Production included services, figures, decorative pieces. Decoration featured landscapes, birds, botanical flowers. Strong Meissen influence. Famous for "flora Danica" pattern reproducing with scientific accuracy flowers and plants of Denmark. *Marks: Cursive letter "F" and an "S" until 1766, then three wavy lines. Modern mark adds crown and name "Royal Copenhagen, Denmark" over three wavy lines.*

COZZI: Founded 1765 by Geminiano Cozzi in Venice, production continuing to 1812. Hard, grayish paste, brilliant glaze. Wide range of production: coffee and teapots, cups, tureens. Floral and chinoiseries decorations; landscapes, figures. Strong colors, excellent gilding. *Marks: Usually a pronged anchor in red.*

DAVENPORT: Factory founded *c.* 1793 in Longport, Staffordshire, England, by John Davenport. Pottery production in early years led to first soft-paste porcelain *c.* 1800. Paste varied from white, translucent body to more grayish hue. Fine body and glaze, with much use of ground colors, i.e., apple green. Pictorial patterns characteristic. Some more ornate, heavily gilded ware, after Derby. *Marks: "Davenport" or "Davenport, Longport," sometimes with anchor. After 1806, "Davenport, Longport, Staffordshire" surrounded by an anchor.* Factory closed 1882.

DERBY: Factory founded in Derby, England, *c.* 1750, by William Duesbury, who had soft-paste production well established by 1756 (and who later purchased Chelsea, 1770, and Bow, 1776). Early Derby paste was soft, warm, creamy white, gradually changing to bone-ash body in Chelsea-Derby period, *c.* 1770–84. Earlier decoration more restrained than later use of gold scrolls and ornate Imari-style patterns. Relatively infrequent use of blue and white. Figures 1755–60 copies of Meissen models, included lively Chinese groups, animals, Four Seasons, much imitation of Chelsea. Silver shapes copied. Excellent biscuit figures from 1770. *Marks: Early marks rare: "D" beneath crown; crossed batons with six dots in 1782. Chelsea-Derby period, 1770–84: "D" over anchor. Robert Bloor period, 1811–48, saw overdecoration with lavish gilding.* Present Royal Crown Derby Porcelain Company established 1876.

DOCCIA: Italian hard-paste factory established 1735 near Florence by Carlo Ginori. First public sale 1746. Family-owned to 1896, then became Richard-Ginori. Coarse, grayish paste with glaze gradually becoming opaque white. Decoration late Baroque. Stylized floral and relief patterns. Wide range of tablewares. Italian comedy and animal figures. Floral decoration in underglaze blue. Stencils, chinoiseries, armorial designs. Large production. *Marks: None first twenty years. Late eighteenth century: star in blue, red, gold, or incised. "Ginori" in eighteenth century. Some Doccia, marked with crown and "N" of old Capodimonte, sold as such in nineteenth century.*

DRESDEN: The English name commonly given to the hard-paste porcelain made at Meissen, in Saxony, Germany, from 1710. Europe's first "true" porcelain, like the Chinese.

FRANKENTHAL: Established 1755 in Mannheim, Germany, with changing management, German and French, according to fortunes of war. Closed 1799–1800, molds going to Nymphenburg and Grunstadt factories. Fine, milklike hard paste. Tablewares and decorative pieces influenced by Meissen, then by Sèvres. Excellent quality, wide range of production, varied and beautiful painting. After 1775 output showed Neoclassical trend, with much gilding. *Marks: Lion rampant in blue. Later, initials of Elector Palatine Karl Theodor interwoven with crown.*

FULDA: Founded 1765 in Hesse, Germany, by the Prince Bishop of Fulda; burned and rebuilt 1767; continued to closing in 1790. Fine quality paste, well-modeled court and pastoral figures. Meissen influence. Style largely Rococo. Tableware with portraits, classical borders, landscapes. *Marks: Double intertwined script "FF" forming an "H," sometimes surrounded by crown and small cross.*

FURSTENBERG: Founded 1747 in Brunswick, Germany. True, hard-paste porcelain dates from 1753. Became private business 1859, continues today. Paste yellowish; glaze grayish, with frequent imperfections. Decoration generally Rococo, after Meissen. Good figure execution. Plaques, busts in biscuit. Best production 1770–90. *Marks: Curving "F" in blue, later with added crown.*

GOTHA: Founded 1757 in Thuringia, Germany, by Wilhelm von Rotberg. Production continues today. Creamy paste. Variety of tablewares and figures. Style largely Louis Seize and Neoclassic. Monochrome landscapes in reddish brown. *Marks: Various single letter "R," or "G" after 1805.*

HEREND: Founded 1839 in Hungary by Vince Stingl and Moritz Fischer. Production largely copies of both Oriental and European factories such as Sèvres. *Marks: Name impressed or Hungarian coat of arms in blue.*

HEWELCKE: *c.* 1758–63. Yellowish paste and dull glaze. Tablewares and figures of medium quality. *Mark: "V" for Venice.* Founder from Dresden.

HÖCHST: Established 1750 near Frankfurt, Germany, under patronage of Elector of Mainz. Production ended 1796. A milk-white hard paste, with light, attractive, Rococo decoration. Figures after Meissen, included Italian comedy series, peasants, pseudo-Chinese groups. Later decoration after Sèvres. *Mark: A wheel, the heraldic sign of Mainz, impressed or painted in various colors.*

KLOSTER-VEILSDORF: Founded 1760 by Prince Friedrich Wilhelm Eugen von Hildburghausen in Thuringia, Germany. Varying success and management, to present. Fine, milk-white paste. Varied production with strong Meissen influence. Tableware, figures, portrait busts. *Mark: "C" and "V" in various combinations. Modern mark is strong "C" and "V" interlocked.*

LIMBACH: Founded 1772 in Thuringia, Germany, by Gotthelf Greiner. Useful wares and figures after Meissen, but much less sophisticated and unevenly executed. *Marks: Crossed "L's"; sometimes a clover leaf.*

LE NOVE: Founded 1752 in Venice by Pasquale Antonibon. Varying fortunes and management until 1835. Grayish paste, glossy glaze. Various tableware, including Rococo teapots; also figures. Decorations were pastoral scenes and figures, harbor scenes, chinoiseries. *Marks: Included initials of founder, "G.B.A."; six-pointed stars; or incised "Nove" on figures.*

LIVERPOOL: Twelve or more small porcelain factories here by *c.* 1760 (at various times), and their production difficult to separate. Generally a soft, coarse soapstone paste, grayish in color. Bluish glaze with bubbles. Richard Chaffers largest producer, 1756–65. John Sadler did considerable transfer printing. Other factories: William Reid and Philip Christian. Decoration after Oriental models in both underglaze blue and other colors, often indistinctly defined. Shapes, including mugs and jugs, after Worcester. Over-all Liverpool production of uneven quality, at best. *Marks: Rare in eighteenth-century Liverpool porcelains. Considerable current research in this area of identification.*

LONGTON HALL: Founded *c.* 1749 by William Jenkinson, joined in 1751 by William Littler. First porcelain factory in Staffordshire, England. History of factory incomplete. Heavy body; soft, glassy paste; waxy glaze; soft colors. Figures in Staffordshire pottery tradition, with flower decoration after Meissen. Useful wares included leaf and fruit forms. Also "Snowman" group with thick glaze. Handles Staffordshire crabstock or strap. Landscapes in pink, purple, green with rushes and flower sprays. *Marks: Rare; two "L's," crossed, in blue.*

LOWESTOFT: Founded 1757 in Lowestoft, Suffolk, England. (The name Lowestoft was for years used incorrectly for Chinese Export or China Trade porcelain. This mistaken usage had no connection with the English Lowestoft factory here discussed.) Soft, phosphatic paste with yellowish tinge. Glaze uneven, dull, often with small specks. Decoration often follows Chinese blue-and-white ware. Silver shapes and numerous mugs, other articles marked "Souvenir" or "Trifle" from Lowestoft. Copies of Bow,

112

Sèvres (French), c. 1761
·Soup dish with stand
*(Courtesy the Wickes Collection,
Museum of Fine Arts,
Boston, Massachusetts)*

Nymphenburg (German), eighteenth century
"Lovers Among the Ruins"
F. A. Bustelli, modeler
(Courtesy the Delhom Collection,
Mint Museum of Art,
Charlotte, North Carolina)

Vienna (Austrian), Du Paquier period,
eighteenth century
White broth bowl
Relief decoration
(Courtesy the Delhom Collection,
Mint Museum of Art,
Charlotte, North Carolina)

Longton Hall (English), c. 1753
Tureen and soup plate
Decorated in "Littler's blue"
*(Courtesy the Campbell Museum
Collection, Camden, New Jersey)*

Chelsea (English), eighteenth century
Pair of figures
*(Courtesy the Delhom Collection,
Mint Museum of Art, Charlotte,
North Carolina)*

ABOVE: Bonnin and Morris (American), c. 1770–1772
Sweetmeat dish
(Courtesy the Smithsonian Institution,
National Museum of History and Technology,
Washington, D.C.)
BELOW: Bonnin and Morris (American), c. 1770–1772
Fruit basket
(Courtesy the Henry Francis du Pont Winterthur Museum,
Winterthur, Delaware)

OVERLEAF: Nymphenburg
(German), c. 1760
Figure of Columbine
F. A. Bustelli, modeler
(Courtesy The Metropolitan
Museum of Art,
New York City)

Chelsea (English), c. 1752–1756
Pair of rabbit tureens
(Courtesy the Campbell Museum
Collection, Camden, New Jersey)

Worcester forms. Some transfer printing in underglaze blue. Sprig decoration later popular. *Marks: Copies of Worcester marks or numerals 1–9 inside foot rims.* Firm name from 1770: Robert Browne & Co. Factory closed in 1802.

LUDWIGSBURG: Founded 1756 by Bonifacius Höchner and taken over in 1758 by Duke Carl Eugen of Württemberg, Germany. Slightly grayish paste, smoky, flamed. Figures of high quality, using much relief. Early production best, before move to Stuttgart in 1776. Closed 1824. *Marks: Various combinations of Duke's initials, sometimes surrounded by crown. Mark used later by nineteenth-century factories.*

MARIEBERG: Founded 1758 near Stockholm, Sweden, by Johann Ehrenreich. Soft-paste porcelain after Mennecy and hard-paste porcelain after 1777; milky white paste; useful shapes; uneven quality. *Marks: Incised "MB" (1766–69). Trio of small coronets over interlocking "A's," in pink.* Factory closed 1758.

MEDICI: 1575–87. Italian soft-paste porcelain made in Florence under patronage of Francesco de Medici, Grand Duke of Tuscany. A white, translucent paste with milky, opaque glaze. Few surviving pieces (about sixty), all in blue. Very rare. *Marks: Dome of Cathedral in Florence, in blue; with or without letter "F"; word "Prova" on one flask in Louvre.*

MEISSEN: At Meissen, near Dresden, Germany, Europe's first true, or hard-paste, porcelain (like the Chinese) was invented or discovered in 1708 under patronage of Augustus, Elector of Saxony, founder and chief customer of Royal Saxon Porcelain Manufactory; commercially produced after *c.* 1713. From early days under Johann Böttger, a gradual development to superb quality in the 1720's. Several notable artists and modelers, headed by Herold and Kaendler. Strong Japanese and Chinese decorative influence. Kakiemon, Rococo relief, Oriental flowers, harbor scenes, chinoiseries, pastorals after Watteau school, and so on. Wide range of table services, figures, other objects. Succession of wars, other problems led to inferior production in nineteenth century. At its best, Meissen porcelain is of unsurpassed quality, with important influence on other Continental and English factories of eighteenth century. *Mark: The famous crossed swords, after 1724. Other marks, i.e., pseudo-Chinese, were used in the 1720's. Early Böttger porcelain was unmarked.*

MENNECY: Established 1734 by Louis-François, Duc de Villeroy. Various owners and locations in Paris area. Closed 1806. One of the best French soft-paste porcelains. Milky white body, brilliant glaze. Decidedly Japanese (Kakiemon) and Chinese influence. Excellent bird, flower, landscape painting. Two characteristic colors: strong green and brownish red. Biscuit ware; figures, especially children; tea services; small items, such as boxes, handles, toilet pots, candlesticks. *Mark: "D.V.," incised or painted in red or blue.*

MINTON: Stoke-on-Trent, England. Founded 1793 by Thomas Minton, with William Pownall and Joseph Poulson. Continued under various

Minton descendants, with associates, becoming Minton, Ltd., in 1883. First soft-paste porcelain produced 1798, but not extensively or profitably until 1825 (none between 1817 and 1823). The leading English porcelain manufactory of the Victorian era. Highly skilled French and English artists and modelers; decidedly Sèvres influence; wide range of high quality, useful and decorative wares. Decoration included Chinese landscapes, gilding, encrusted floral modeling, painted flowers. *Marks: Earlier porcelain generally unmarked, so often attributed to other factories. Marks of crossed "L's" and crossed swords sometimes used after Sèvres and Meissen.*

NANTGARW: Established 1813 by William Billingsley and Samuel Walker in Glamorgan, Wales. Short-lived and largely experimental factory was near Swansea, 1814–17. Extremely white soft-paste with soft, thick glaze. Very translucent. Tablewares, tea and dessert services. Much decoration after Sèvres, often executed in London. Financial problems ended in purchase of plant and molds by John Rose of Coalport, 1822, after 1819 closing. Superb quality porcelain. *Mark: Impressed "Nantgarw" over letters "C.W."*

NAPLES: Established by King Ferdinand IV of Naples, first at Potici, 1771, then at the Palace in Naples, 1773. Services made for diplomatic presentation, 1780. Sold 1807, moved, and after production declined, closed in 1834. Models purchased by C. L. Ginori. A translucent, glassy soft-paste with thin glaze. Shapes and decoration Rococo, later Classical. Local scenes, Vesuvius, animals, hunting, and so on. Figures few and not first rate. *Mark: Crown over letter "N," in red, blue, or impressed.*

NEWHALL: Established 1781 in Shelton, Staffordshire, England, by a syndicate with changing membership. Early hard paste was milk white with glittering glaze; converted to soft-paste bone-china formula after 1810. Average quality. Decoration included sprigged-muslin pattern; baskets and wreaths of flowers, shells. Gilded ware, relief hunting scenes, printed landscapes. *Marks: Letter "N" incised, and later "Newhall," transfer printed in italics. Double circle enclosing words "New Hall" on bone china (1810–25).* Factory closed 1825.

NYMPHENBURG: Factory established 1747 at Neudeck, Germany, removed to Nymphenburg in 1761. First successful porcelain, 1753. Finely painted tablewares, but chiefly famous for beautifully modeled figures by sculptor Franz Anton Bustelli, whose Italian comedy figures and Chinese groups are considered by many collectors to be unsurpassed in the eighteenth century. Factory leased to Albert Bäuml in 1862 and is still in existence, continuing to make fine copies of early Bustelli figures. *Marks: Checkered Bavarian shield, impressed.*

PARIS: General term for numerous small porcelain factories that developed in Paris area with relaxation of strict Sèvres monopoly and discovery of kaolin deposits in France. By end of eighteenth century, most Paris porcelain was of a highly vitrified hard paste and extremely white. Classical designs and much gilt. Examples: Clignancourt, 1771–98 (*Marks: Windmill and crowned "M," or "M"*); Rue de Bondy, 1780–1829 (*Mark: "AG"*

122

with or without crown); La Courtille, established 1773 (*Mark: Crossed torches in underglaze blue, or incised*); Faubourg Saint-Denis, established 1771 (*Mark: Crossed pipes, or "C.P." crowned—1779–93*). Note: Most Paris factories had royal or noble sponsors.

PINXTON: Founded 1796 in Pinxton, Derbyshire, England, by William Billingsley and John Coke. Closed *c.* 1813. Produced translucent soft-paste porcelain. Paste coarser, more opaque after 1801. Tableware decorated with characteristic flower sprigs on white ground, landscapes. *Marks: Rare. Small arrow over "190"; half moon with star; vertical arrow in outline; word "Pinxton."*

PLYMOUTH: Established 1768 by William Cookworthy. Transferred to Bristol, England, in 1770. Financial problems after 1775; sold 1781. Important as first English hard-paste porcelain; white, hard, translucent. The glaze, grayish, often with bubbles—dull, thick. Frequent flaws and discolorations. Figures after Longton Hall. Sets of "Seasons" and "Continents." Decoration after Derby and Worcester. Some good landscape painting in Sèvres style. Useful wares after silver shapes. Colors have cloudy, smoky tint. *Marks: The Arabic symbol for tin—a combined "2" and "4." Also "T" and "To."*

ROCKINGHAM: Established 1820 in Swinton, Yorkshire, England (at site of an old pottery) by Thomas Brameld, who was joined by Earl Fitzwilliam after 1826. Factory closed 1842. High quality bone porcelain with creamy color, dense texture. Clear, brilliant, well-distributed glaze. Beautiful ground colors: green, blue, yellow, pink. Decoration included named views in reserve panels: cottages, castles, and so on. Rococo style, after Coalport. Large tea-service production. Increasing tendency to overdecoration in poor taste. *Marks: "Rockingham Works, Brameld" or "Royal Rockingham Works, Brameld," printed or impressed with addition, after 1826, of Earl Fitzwilliam's griffin, painted in red or impressed.*

ROUEN: Early French soft paste, of uneven quality, made 1673–96 by Louis Poterat. Followed shapes from silver- and goldsmiths. Services, vases, cups without handles. Most decoration blue and white from pottery models. *Marks: Few. A rare "A.P." with star or rowel may be Saint-Cloud.*

RUSSIAN: A number of porcelain factories from 1744, including Imperial Factory at St. Petersburg, established 1758 (*Marks: Imperial monograms and emblems*); Gardner, established 1766, Moscow (*Mark: "G" in eighteenth century*); Popov, established 1806. Shapes and decoration after German, French factories.

SAINT-CLOUD: Founded *c.* 1677 at Seine-et-Oise, France, near Versailles, as faience factory by Pierre Chicaneau under patronage of King Louis XIV's brother, Duke of Orleans. First successful French soft-paste porcelain produced here by 1693. Various managements, to closing in 1766. Paste yellowish or creamy ivory with fine glaze. *Marks: Sun with rays or letters "St. C." with "T"; also, 1722–66, letters "St. C. St. Tron."*

SAMSON: A French manufacturer of hard-paste porcelain, long specializing in reproductions of Chinese Export, English soft-paste porcelain, and Continental factories; also enamel, pottery. Sometimes marks of originals also reproduced. Established 1845 and still in business in Paris.

SÈVRES: Soft-paste factory, successor to Vincennes, moved to Sèvres, near Paris, in 1756. Louis XV took one-third interest in 1753. Always a luxury product for royal or court use, sale, and presentation. Periods: Monarchy (1756–93); Louis XV, XVI; First Republic (1793–1804); First Empire (1805–15). Soft-paste was warm, pure white. Discovery of kaolin in Limoges district led to first hard-paste porcelain at Sèvres *c.* 1768. Hard paste only was produced at factory (*c.* 1769–1847), when soft paste was reintroduced in Sèvres production. Sèvres achieved a high level of excellence in the 1770's and 1780's. Table services, large tureens, presentation objects showed Meissen and Japanese influence in earlier years. Developed beautiful ground colors: jaune jonquille, rose Pompadour, bleu-de-roi, and so on. After *c.* 1760, Sèvres surpassed Meissen as the leading porcelain influence. *Marks: 1756–93. A system of single and double alphabetical letters inside crossed "L's"; i.e., "G" is 1759, "GG" is 1784, and so on.*

SPODE: Founded 1770 in Stoke-on-Trent, Staffordshire, England, by Josiah Spode, to manufacture faience. First porcelain produced here *c.* 1800. Factory important for its high technical quality, for advances in mechanization of manufacture, for its improvement of transfer printing process, and for its perfection of a sound basic formula for bone china. Tea, dinner, dessert services; Chinese and Imari patterns; landscapes in reserve panels; tendency to excessive decoration. William Copeland purchased factory 1833. After various ownerships, factory became W. T. Copeland and Son. *Marks: "Spode" in various forms.*

SWANSEA: Founded 1764 in Glamorgan, Wales, as Cambrian Pottery Works, by William Coles. Porcelain produced *c.* 1814–17. Early "duck egg" or greenish body later replaced, first by a yellowish, then whitish paste. Body became harder, more durable. Decoration shows decidedly French influence, with flowers from botanical prints. Tableware most common production. *Marks: "Swansea" impressed or printed in red. After 1817, trident often impressed, with other marks.*

SWITZERLAND: Soft-paste porcelain was made briefly at Zurich *c.* 1763–65. Hard-paste porcelain was made also at Zurich, to 1790. Other centers for hard-paste production were Geneva, late eighteenth century, and Nyon, established 1780. *Mark: Fish in underglaze blue.*

TUCKER: American porcelain factory established 1826–27 by William Tucker in Philadelphia. Various partners, including Hulme, Hemphills. Closed 1838. Strong, well-fired body. Long thought to be hard paste, almost certain to be a bone china. Forms generally classical. Decoration varied from simple sepia to elaborate gilt and polychrome. Urns done in Greco-Roman style, like Paris porcelain. Tea and dinner services, pitchers. *Marks: Few; incised initials.*

VEZZI: Factory founded 1720, closed *c.* 1728, by Francesco Vezzi, goldsmith. Hard-paste porcelain equaled Meissen, but quality varied. Production included decorations, cups, teapots. *Marks: "Venezio" or "Vena" in various forms, in red, blue, gold.*

VICKERS: An American porcelain made briefly (*c.* 1824) in Chester County, Pennsylvania, by John Vickers. *Marks: Sometimes "John Vickers," with date, e.g., "1824."*

VIENNA: Europe's second hard-paste factory, established 1719 in Vienna by Claude du Paquier, aided by workmen lured from Meissen. Early paste smoky with a clear glaze. Baroque shapes after silver forms and Meissen. Decorations tended to be abstract, panels, scrolls, trellis designs, hunting and battle subjects. Factory acquired by state, 1744. Active production period under Konrad von Sorgenthal, 1784–1805. Declining fortunes until eventual closing, 1864. *Marks: None in du Paquier era. After 1744, a shield in various shapes.* Best of Vienna, superb quality porcelain.

VINCENNES: Established 1738, French soft paste. Predecessor of Sèvres, where factory moved *c.* 1756. Factory purchased 1759 by King Louis XV. Japanese, Meissen influence. Painstaking potting; firing produced deep, soft glaze; nearly perfect soft paste. Early Vincennes had somewhat coarse, grayish body and clear glaze. Flower painting, French in character. *Mark: Usually crossed "L's".*

VIVINIS: Paris firm reproducing earlier wares, especially Chinese Export porcelains. *Mark: Usually square, Chinese-looking character, in red.*

WEDGWOOD: The English factory developed by Josiah Wedgwood starting in 1762. Production included fine creamware, basalt, jasper, and even some porcelain (1812–22). High quality and inexpensive production of creamware made the Wedgwood factory famous and prosperous.

WEESP: Established in North Holland in 1757; closed in 1768. Production largely for decoration, little for everyday use. Generally high quality. Considerable use of relief decoration and scale patterns in rocaille. *Mark: Crossed daggers (points down) intersected by three dots. Also, the letter "W" in underglaze blue or scratched into body.*

WORCESTER: Established 1751 in Worcester, England, by Dr. Wall and associates. Period to 1783 considered best quality. Creamy soapstone body, soft glaze. Fine range of ground colors: scale blue, yellow, apple green. Extensive use of reserve panels with exotic birds. Excellent blue-and-white and transfer printing. Strong Oriental influence in decoration. Considerable production of armorial services, pierced baskets, silver shapes. Figures rare. Successive owners: Flight and Barr, 1792–1807; Barr, Flight, and Barr, 1807–13; Flight, Barr, and Barr, 1813–40; Chamberlain & Co., 1840; Chamberlain's Worcester, 1848. Present Royal Worcester Porcelain Factory established 1862. *Early Marks: Crescent in blue, also square Chinese fret mark.*

APPENDIXES

CHRONOLOGY

1122–249 B.C. Chou dynasty	Chinese learn to glaze pottery.
206 B.C.–A.D. 220 Han dynasty	Proto-porcelain or first porcellaneous ware.
618–906 T'ang dynasty	First true, hard-paste, resonant porcelain.
960–1279 Sung dynasty	Celadons and white translucent Ting ware. Peak era of Chinese ceramics.
c. 1271	Marco Polo at the court of Kublai Khan first sees vessels resembling "porcella," or cowrie shell. (Polo's travel account written 1298–99.)
1280–1368 Yüan dynasty	First white porcelain with underglaze blue decoration, using cobalt.
1368–1644 Ming dynasty	Monochrome wares, overglaze enamels, and blue-and-white porcelains. Extensive export to Middle East, where pottery shows Chinese influence.
1517	First Portuguese ship arrives in Chinese river harbor of Canton.
1557	Portuguese establish trading post in Macao, near Hong Kong.
1575–87	Medici in Florence encourage manufacture of soft-paste porcelain with blue decoration.
c. 1616	First real porcelain manufacture in Japan, after Chinese and Korean influences.
1599/1600	Charter issued in London to "The Governor and Company of Merchants of Trading into the East Indies." Also, the Dutch in Japan.
1602	Dutch East India Company founded. First cargo of porcelain arrives in Holland for public auction after seizure of Portuguese carrack at sea.
1624–61	Dutch conduct China trade from a Formosan base.
1640–46	Japanese add polychrome enamels to porcelain decoration, i.e., Kakiemon, Imari.
1604–57	Over 3 million pieces of Oriental porcelain reach Europe, chiefly through port of Amsterdam.
1662–1722	Reign of Chinese Emperor K'ang Hsi. Peak of Export porcelain trade. European merchants permitted to establish seasonal trading offices, or hongs, in Canton.
1664	French organize Compagnie des Indes Orientales. First shipment of Oriental porcelain arrives in France after 1700.
17th–18th cs.	Many attempts made in Europe to imitate Chinese porcelain in white glazed faience with blue decoration.
1673	Soft-paste porcelain made in Rouen, France, from a

	formula substituting ground glass for kaolin. Production ceased 1696.
1673	Ching-tê-Chên destroyed (again in 1853).
1677	Successful soft-paste porcelain made in Saint-Cloud, near Paris; production in full operation by 1700, continuing until 1766.
1689	Louis XIV has table silver melted down, to be replaced by porcelain.
c. 1708	Europe's first true, hard-paste porcelain made in Dresden by Johann Böttger, after long experimentation.
1710	Founding of the Royal Saxon Porcelain Manufactory by Augustus the Strong and its transfer to Meissen.
1712	Famous letters of Jesuit Father d'Entrecolles reporting on porcelain manufacturing center at Ching-tê-Chên, in Kiangsi province in China, and mentioning kaolin as a key ingredient—for the first time.
1715	English establish trading hong in Canton.
1719	French Compagnie des Deux Indes founded.
1718–19	Important porcelain factory, Europe's second hard-paste, established in Vienna by du Paquier, with help of workmen from Meissen.
1720	Vezzi factory established in Venice. Johann Herold begins important career at Meissen.
1723–35	Yung Chêng reign of Ch'ing dynasty.
c. 1725	Soft-paste factory founded in Chantilly, near Paris.
1728	French hong established in Canton.
1731	Famous Meissen modeler of figures, Johann Kaendler, begins his celebrated and much copied work.
1732	Swedes lease hong in Canton.
1735	Porcelain factories established in Mennecy, France, and Doccia, near Florence, Italy.
1736–95	Ch'ien Lung reign of Ch'ing dynasty.
1738	Soft-paste factory begun at Vincennes, predecessor of Sèvres.
1743	Italian factory of Capodimonte established.
c. 1745	Important English soft-paste factory established in Chelsea.
1746	Beginning of German factory at Höchst.
c. 1748	England's Bow factory begins production after 1744 patent.
1750	Introduction of tea drinking to England accelerated, with chocolate and coffee, demand for porcelain.
1751	English factories of Worcester and Derby established.
1755–56	German factory of Frankenthal established in Mannheim.
1753	Nymphenburg, German factory, established.
1754–1763	Bustelli creates his superb figures at Nymphenburg.
1756	French factory of Vincennes moved to Sèvres.
1757	English porcelain factory established in Lowestoft.
1758	Ludwigsburg, Germany, begins factory operation.

127

1759	First successful Dutch porcelain factory started at Weesp.
1759	Porcelain factory established in Copenhagen, Denmark.
1760	Twelve factories making porcelain in Liverpool, England, by this date.
1761	Second porcelain factory in Berlin, Germany, established.
1762	Dutch establish trading post in Canton.
1763	Swiss porcelain factory opens in Zurich.
1768	England's first hard-paste factory opens in Plymouth, moving to Bristol in 1770.
1769	Hard-paste porcelain first made in Sèvres, France.
1770	Chelsea factory purchased by William Duesbury, of Derby. Chelsea-Derby period: 1770–84.
1772	Porcelain factory established in Caughley, England.
1769–72	First American porcelain factory established by Bonnin and Morris in Philadelphia.
1784–85	First voyage of an American ship, *The Empress of China,* to Canton, returning with porcelain as part of cargo.
1796	English porcelain factory of Coalport established in Shropshire.
1827	Tucker porcelain factory established in Philadelphia.

Note: By 1825, the manufacture of porcelain had reached full commercial production. The great days of individually created and decorated pieces were nearly over and so, too, the story of what we think of as "antique porcelain." From here on, porcelain, once an art, becomes a business.

GLOSSARY

A

ARITA: Japanese area, Hizen province, where Japanese porcelain was made in some forty factories and from which much of the Japanese Imari porcelain was shipped. Arita production included blue and white, pierced ware, low relief, celadon colored enamels.

ARMORIAL: Porcelain service and individual pieces decorated to order with coats of arms and crests from families, organizations. Chiefly made in Chinese Export eighteenth-century porcelain. Decoration done from engravings or sketches sent to China. Several thousand separate arms have been identified. Portugal, England, other European countries were major buyers of this type; America a minor market.

B

BISCUIT: Unglazed, fired porcelain body, before decoration. Groups of figures were sometimes left in biscuit form. Biscuit was also decorated in relief, for example, Chinese blanc de Chine of Fukien.

BLANC DE CHINE: White unpainted porcelain first made in the province of Fukien, China. Widely copied in Europe. Often decorated in relief, e.g., the prunus motif.

BLUE AND WHITE: The Chinese and Japanese decorated porcelain that was the earliest and most popular export to Europe, inspiring imitations in all major factories, including the blue-and-white earthenware of Germany, Holland (Delft), England.

BONE PORCELAIN: The standard English porcelain since 1800. Basically hard-paste, with as much as 40 per cent bone ash (calcined bones of animals) added. Some bone ash used as early as 1749, at Bow—also at Chelsea, Lowestoft, Derby.

C

CANN: Usually a coffee can or cup in cylindrical shape.

CANTON: Name given relatively recently to a pattern of underglaze blue-and-white porcelain of the late eighteenth and nineteenth centuries. It was made largely at Ching-tê-Chên but shipped abroad through river port of Canton—hence the name. Pattern usually included river scene, island, trees, bridges, boats, and figures in varying arrangement. Canton ware made up bulk of Chinese porcelain exported to Europe.

CELADON: A porcellaneous ware of a pale, soft shade of green, resembling jade. Known from ninth century by Persians and Chinese by other names. Word became current in eighteenth century; was probably derived from a seventeenth-century French pastoral romance based on a conception of Saladin, twelfth-century sultan of Egypt.

CERAMIC: From the Greek "keramos," or clay, so applied to anything made of fired clay. The potters' area in Athens was called "Keramikos."

CHINA CLAY: A white-burning refractory clay produced by decomposition of feldspathic rock. An essential ingredient of hard-paste porcelain, called "kaolin" by Chinese.

CHINOISERIES: Fanciful, pseudo-Oriental interpretations of Chinese scenes and other subjects—an extremely popular decoration on eighteenth-century European porcelains.

CRACKLE: A network or pattern of cracks set up by uneven expansion and contraction of glaze and body in cooling process. Can occur intentionally or by accident of firing conditions, chemical content of body, and so on.

CRAZE: Somewhat like crackle, a surface of cracks or lines caused by the china's being withdrawn from kiln before it has cooled, or by some other defect in firing process.

CREAMWARE: The commercially successful, high quality earthenware perfected by Josiah Wedgwood and other eighteenth-century Staffordshire potters. Widely exported to Continent and America.

D

DELFT: Tin-enameled earthenware made in Delft, Holland, in seventeenth and eighteenth centuries. Name, with small "d," also given to similar ware made in England at Bristol, London, and Liverpool. Most delftware is decorated in blue-and-white or polychrome design.

DIAPERED: Scalloped border decoration.

E

EARTHENWARE: See POTTERY.

EGG SHELL: Paper-thin, white Chinese porcelain, called "t'o T'ai," or "bodiless," ware, first made in reign of Yung Lo (Ming dynasty) and later copied in reigns of K'ang Hsi and Yung Chêng (Ch'ing dynasty).

ENAMELS: Vitreous overglaze pigments made from metallic oxides that fuse when fired at a relatively low temperature (about 750° C.)

EXPORT PORCELAIN: Chinese and Japanese porcelain made to foreign specifications: special shapes and decorations to order. Chinese Export was usually delivered at Canton through Chinese agents or hong merchants. At one time or another, at least a dozen foreign nations maintained eighteenth- and nineteenth-century headquarters for such trading in tea, porcelain, and other commodities. Much of this ware was decorated in China, relatively little in Europe. Quality varied enormously, but the Chinese generally looked upon Export porcelain as inferior to that made for

Chinese use. Chinese Export porcelain is sometimes referred to as China Trade Porcelain but should not be called Lowestoft, a persistent error.

F

FAIENCE: A French term applied to tin-glazed earthenware. A major industry in the sixteenth, seventeenth, and eighteenth centuries, but virtually ruined by competition from superior English creamware.

FAMILLE JAUNE: Chinese porcelain of the K'ang Hsi through Ch'ien Lung reigns (1662–1795), with a dominant yellow decorative pattern.

FAMILLE NOIRE: Chinese porcelain of the K'ang Hsi through Ch'ien Lung reigns, with a dominant black decorative pattern, usually combined with green.

FAMILLE ROSE: Chinese porcelain pattern of an opaque pink color that came to China from Europe (Leyden) in the reign of K'ang Hsi, and was more fully developed in subsequent reign of Yung Chêng. Derives from a combination of gold chloride and tin.

FAMILLE VERTE: Chinese porcelain of K'ang Hsi and subsequent reigns featuring a dominant brilliant copper green. Pattern also used manganese purple, antimony yellow, cobalt blue, iron red.

FELDSPAR: Any of a group of aluminum silicates with potassium, calcium, or barium. Usually white or pinkish, feldspar comprises about 25 per cent of porcelain ingredients and under heat fires to a sort of natural glass.

FITZHUGH: A popular design on Chinese Export porcelain. A trellis-work border decorated with four cut pomegranates and flying butterflies, completed by branches and the Greek fret. Pattern occurs in at least seven colors—green, blue, and orange being the most common.

FLUORESCENCE: The reaction of certain substances under ultraviolet light. Useful in revealing repairs, also in the separation of hard and soft pastes and in the identification of pastes characteristic of a few individual factories.

FRIT: A ground-glass ingredient of some soft-paste porcelains used as substitute for kaolin of true porcelain. Mixture may include sand, saltpeter, glass, soda, salt, chalk, alum—in varying combinations. Usually ground and then mixed with clay.

FUKIEN or BLANC DE CHINE (PAI TZU): Name given to creamy white seventeenth- and eighteenth-century Chinese porcelain made at Te-hua in Fukien province, about one hundred miles south of Chien-yang. Best is of a rich, lustrous, glossy nature; extremely beautiful.

G

GILDING: The application of gold decoration to porcelain by various processes, such as mixing with honey, mercury, and so on, before firing. The English and Dutch often added gilding to porcelain imported from the Orient.

GLAZES: Porcelain's glasslike outer layer—with decoration added under or over it at varying temperatures.

GRISAILLE: A style of painting, using various shades of gray, to create an effect of bas-relief.

H

HAUSMALEREI: A German term for porcelain decorated outside the factory—at home or in small shops—by individual artists. A popular practice at both Meissen and Vienna.

HONG: Factories or trading buildings located in the restricted foreign-concession area of Canton. Here eighteenth-century Western nations completed their transactions with the Chinese hong merchants. Foreigners both lived and did business in these three-story buildings during the annual trading season.

I

IRONSTONE: A durable, heavy type of English earthenware, largely produced in Staffordshire during the nineteenth century; e.g., Mason's Ironstone.

IMARI: Japanese porcelain patterns produced in seventeenth and eighteenth centuries and decorated in strong reds, blues, golds, perhaps derived from brocade textile patterns. Name taken from Hizen province port from which this Arita-area porcelain was shipped. Not made at Imari. Patterns widely copied in Europe and even by the Chinese, in the eighteenth and nineteenth centuries.

J

JESUIT: A term used for religious decorations applied to eighteenth-century Chinese Export porcelain, usually in black, from European engravings. Incorrectly used to describe "pencil" wares in black and gold.

K

KAKIEMON: A fine seventeenth- and eighteenth-century Japanese porcelain that took its name from a family of potters. Restrained decoration of flowers, trees, insects, birds, dragons. Widely admired and copied by Meissen, English and French factories, even Chinese.

KAOLIN: The basic ingredient of true porcelain. A clay composed of various combinations of silicates that resist fusion. It fires white and opaque, and withstands high temperatures. Name derived from hills near Ching-tê-Chên.

KUTANI: Japanese porcelain made *c.* 1650–1750 in Kaga province. Average quality body but good decoration, using an intense blue, green, yellow, and purple.

L

LOWESTOFT: An English soft-paste porcelain made at Lowestoft, England (1757–1802), *not,* as too often thought, a correct name for porcelain made in China for export.

M

MAIOLICA: Another name for faience or Continental (usually Italian) tin-glazed earthenware.

MANDARIN: Chinese polychrome, decorated porcelain featuring distinctive medallion or "rose medallion" device. A deterioration of famille rose; developed after 1812 and probaby produced at or near Canton.

MOONS: Bright circular patches in some English and French porcelains; visible with transmitted light and apparently resulting from bubbles in the paste.

N

NANKING: A pattern of Chinese blue-and-white underglaze porcelain made for export at Ching-tê-Chên, but taking its name from the important shipping center of Nanking. Nanking and Canton differ chiefly in border designs; the former being "spearhead" and the latter "scalloped." Later Nanking was often embellished with gold outlines, or accents.

O

ONION PATTERN: An eighteenth-century Meissen pattern derived from a Chinese design incorporating not an onion but a pomegranate. Copied by a number of other European factories. Many modern reproductions.

P

PASTE, HARD: True porcelain as it originated in China and rediscovered at Meissen, Germany, in the eighteenth century. See *Porcelain.*

PÂTE DURE: French hard-paste porcelain.

PÂTE-SUR-PÂTE: Low-relief designs applied in slip on unfired ceramics —with many layers, giving a semi-translucent effect. Final result was sharpened further by carving. Best known at Minton, from work of Marc Solon.

PÂTE TENDRE: A French term for artificial, or soft-paste, porcelain— made from clay and ground glass.

PASTE, SOFT: Artificial, or soft-paste, porcelain made by mixing white clay with ground glass or some other ingredient such as bone ash or soapstone. The glazing of artificial porcelain was done at a second firing. Fired at lower temperatures than true porcelain, soft paste is less plastic and more difficult to handle. Colored enamels tend to sink into artificial porcelain, whereas in true porcelain they tend to remain on top of the glaze. Soft-paste porcelain is generally warmer and more luminous than hard paste.

PENTUNTSE: The Chinese word "pai-tun-tzê" means little white blocks of clay. A feldspathic rock that in ground form is one of the two principal ingredients of true porcelain, the other being kaolin.

PORCELAIN: Hard-paste, or true, porcelain was once generally referred to as "china" by English-speaking peoples, but was called porcelain by most Continental peoples. Porcelain is a hard, white, fine-textured, resonant, acid-resistant, impervious, low-heat-conducting material that is usually translucent. It is the highest grade product in the field of ceramics, and is generally composed of about 50 per cent of slowly fusible or nonfusible kaolin, 25 per cent of quartz, and about 25 per cent feldspar, which under high temperature forms a fusible glass and acts as a flux. The relative amounts of the three ingredients vary according to the texture desired; the more kaolin, the harder the porcelain. (Today "china" means just about anything in the pottery field, hard or soft.)

PORCELLA: The highly polished cowrie shell from which Marco Polo derived the name "porcellana," i.e., porcelain. Europeans did not use the term porcelain generally until the sixteenth century, and then it referred to Ming ware, which was both white and translucent.

POTTERY: Usually refers to all classes of baked-clay wares with the exception of stoneware and porcelains. Pottery is a clay having the following characteristics when fired: It (1) is porous, (2) can be scratched with a steel knife, (3) is opaque, (4) is usually reddish brown, yellow, brown, or gray, depending upon the composition. Some pottery is baked in the sun rather than fired.

PROTO PORCELAIN: Chinese stoneware with green-gray celadon glaze. Han period.

R

ROSE MEDALLION: See page 31, and also, MANDARIN.

S

SALOPIAN: One mark used on English Caughley porcelain of eighteenth century. Name derives from Salop, in Shropshire, where factory was located.

SALTGLAZE: Stoneware given a thin, rough, glassy glaze by throwing salt into the kiln during firing.

SCALE GROUNDS: Decoration of porcelain made in design of overlapping, fishlike scales.

SHARDS or SHERDS: Broken pieces of pottery or porcelain, useful for comparisons and study.

SLIP DECORATION: A primitive method of decorating pottery by trailing liquid clay (slip) over an earthenware body into free-form designs.

SPRIGGING: The application of small molded relief decoration to the surface of porcelain by use of liquid clay, or "slip."

SPUR MARK: Marks left on bases of porcelains where piece has rested on small spurs, or supports, during firing.

STAFFORDSHIRE: The general name given to earthenware made by many factories in this area of England. Some porcelain was also produced here under specific factory name.

STONEWARE: A semi-porcellaneous type of ware fired at high temperatures. Generally nonporous, fused, glassy, resistant to scratching, less resonant than true porcelain; sometimes semi-translucent.

T

TRANSFER PRINTING: A process of decorating porcelain that involves applying colors into the lines of a copper plate, then pressing a wet, thin paper onto the copper, thus "transferring" the etching to the porcelain surface in color, after which the piece is refired to fix the decoration. Originated at Battersea *c.* 1753, and introduced at Worcester factory, 1757, on glaze, later underglaze. Several colors used, including black, puce, blue. This was probably England's major contribution in the field of porcelain decoration.

TZU: An approximate transliteration of the Chinese general term for porcelain, implying something of a quality of resonance. "Pai-tzu" adds the quality of whiteness.

W

WASTERS: Rejects from the kiln, pieces damaged in firing.

WILLOW PATTERN: An English mixture of Chinese elements: buildings in the center, a prominent willow tree, and two or three figures crossing a bridge, with doves overhead. A fence crosses foreground and a Chinese-style border surrounds everything. Pattern probably originated with Staffordshire potters; widely copied throughout the nineteenth century and usually transfer printed.

BIBLIOGRAPHY

The following bibliography is meant to provide the new collector or student of porcelain with a basic, current, and reliable frame of reference. Most of these books have more extensive bibliographies in their special fields. Care has been taken to include a number of volumes containing fine printing and color reproduction. Naturally, there are many other well-documented sources of information: catalogues of special exhibitions and collections, proceedings of organizations such as the English Ceramic Circle, and catalogues of important auctions or other sales. Each collector will gradually acquire the kind of reference library that best suits his special interests and needs.

Here, at least, is a sound beginning.

GENERAL

Backlin-Landman, Hedy, and Edna Shapiro
  The Story of Porcelain
  New York: The Odyssey Press, Inc., 1965
Boger, Louise Ade
  The Dictionary of World Pottery and Porcelain
  New York: Charles Scribner's Sons, 1971
Charleston, R. J., ed.
  World Ceramics: An Illustrated History
  New York: McGraw-Hill, Inc., 1968
Cox, Warren E.
  The Book of Pottery and Porcelain
  New York: Crown Publishers, Inc., 1944
Litchfield, Frederick
  Pottery and Porcelain: A Guide for Collectors, 5th ed., rev. by Frank
    Tilley
  New York: M. Barrows and Company, 1951
Savage, George
  Porcelain Through the Ages, 2d ed.
  Baltimore: Penguin Books, 1963. Paperback survey
Weiss, Gustav
  The Book of Porcelain
  Translated by Janet Seligman
  New York: Praeger Publishers, Inc., 1971

PORCELAIN MARKS

Chaffers, William
  *Marks and Monograms on European and
    Oriental Pottery and Porcelain,* 15th ed., rev.
  London: W. Reeves, 1965
Cushion, J. P., and W. B. Honey
  Handbook of Pottery and Porcelain Marks, 3d ed., rev.
  London: Faber and Faber, Ltd., 1965
Godden, Geoffrey A.
  *The Handbook of British Pottery and
    Porcelain Marks*
  New York: Frederick A. Praeger, Inc., 1968

Kovel, Ralph M. and Terry H.
  Dictionary of Marks: Pottery and Porcelain
  New York: Crown Publishers, Inc., 1953
Thorn, C. J.
  Handbook of Old Pottery and Porcelain
    Marks
  New York: Tudor Publishing Company, 1947

ORIENTAL

Beurdeley, Michel
  Chinese Trade Porcelain
  Rutland, Vt., and Tokyo: Charles E. Tuttle Company, 1962
Du Boulay, Anthony
  Chinese Porcelain
  Pleasures and Treasures Series
  New York: G. P. Putnam's Sons, 1963
Garner, Sir Harry
  Oriental Blue and White
  New York: Praeger Publishers, Inc., 1970
Honey, William B.
  The Ceramic Art of China and Other
    Countries of the Far East
  New York: The Beechhurst Press, 1954
Hyde, J. A. Lloyd
  Oriental Lowestoft, Chinese Export
    Porcelain, Porcelaine de la Cie des Indes, 2d ed.
  Newport, Monmouthshire, England: Ceramic Book Company, 1964
Jenyns, Soame
  Japanese Porcelain
  New York: Frederick A. Praeger, Inc., 1965
Jenyns, Soame
  Later Chinese Porcelain: The Ch'ing Dynasty—
    1644–1912, 2d ed.
  London: Faber and Faber, Ltd., 1959
Koyama, Fujio, and John Figess
  Two Thousand Years of Oriental Ceramics
  New York: Harry N. Abrams, Inc. (n.d.)
Mudge, Jean McClure
  Chinese Export Porcelain for the American
    Trade (1785–1835)
  Newark, Del.: University of Delaware Press, 1962
Munsterberg, Hugo
  The Ceramic Art of Japan
  Rutland, Vt., and Tokyo: Charles E. Tuttle Company, 1964, 1971
    (3rd printing)
Philips, John Goldsmith
  China Trade Porcelain
  Cambridge, Mass.: Harvard University Press, 1956
Staehlin, Walter A.
  The Book of Porcelain
  New York: The Macmillan Company, 1966. A set of thirty-four
    watercolors depicting the manufacturing, transportation, and sale
    of export porcelain in China in the eighteenth century.

CONTINENTAL

Bacci, Mina
European Porcelain
London: Paul Hamlyn, 1969

Charles, Rollo
Continental Porcelain of the 18th Century
London: Ernest Benn Limited, 1964

Hackenbroch, Yvonne
Meissen and Other Continental Porcelain
The Collection of Irwin Untermayer
Cambridge, Mass.: Harvard University Press, 1956. Published for the
Metropolitan Museum of Art, New York

Ducret, S.
German Porcelain and Faience
New York: Universe Books, 1962

Gautier, Serge, ed.
Les Porcelainiers du XVIII Siècle Français
Paris: Librairie Hachette, 1964

Haggar, Reginald G.
*The Concise Encyclopedia of Continental
Pottery and Porcelain*
New York: Hawthorn Books, 1960

Honey, W. B.
*European Ceramic Art from the End of the Middle
Ages to About 1815,* vol. 1, *An Illustrated Historical Survey*
London: Faber and Faber, Ltd., 1949

Honey, William B.
Dresden China
Troy, N.Y.: David Rosenfeld, 1946

Honey, William B.
French Porcelain of the 18th Century
New York: Pitman Publishing Corporation (n.d.)

Landais, Hubert
French Porcelain
New York: G. P. Putnam's Sons, 1961

Lane, Arthur
Italian Porcelain
London: Faber and Faber, Ltd., 1954

Morley-Fletcher, Hugo
Antique Porcelain in Color: Meissen
New York: Doubleday & Company, Inc., 1971

Wynter, Harriet
An Introduction to European Porcelain
New York: Thomas Y. Crowell Company, 1972

ENGLISH

Barrett, Franklin A.
Worcester Porcelain
New York: Pitman Publishing Corporation (n.d.)

Bemrose, Geoffrey
19th Century English Pottery and Porcelain
London: Faber and Faber, Ltd., 1952

Charleston, R. J., ed.
    English Porcelain, 1745–1850
    London: Ernest Benn Limited, 1965
Hackenbroch, Yvonne
    Chelsea and Other English Porcelain,
        Pottery and Enamel
    The Collection of Irwin Untermayer
    Cambridge, Mass.: Harvard University Press, 1957. Published for the
        Metropolitan Museum of Art, New York.
Dixon, J. L.
    English Porcelain of the 18th Century
    London: Faber and Faber, Ltd., 1952
Fisher, Stanley W.
    English Blue and White Porcelain
        of the 18th Century
    London: B. T. Batsford, Ltd., 1947
Gilhespy, F. Brayshaw
    Derby Porcelain
    London: Spring Books, The Hamlyn Publishing Group, Ltd., 1965
Godden, Geoffrey A.
    Caughley and Worcester Porcelains (1775–1800)
    London: Herbert Jenkins, 1969
Godden, Geoffrey A.
    An Illustrated Encyclopedia of British Pottery and
        Porcelain
    New York: Crown Publishers, Inc., 1966
Godden, Geoffrey A.
    The Illustrated Guide to Lowestoft
        Porcelain
    New York: Frederick A. Praeger, Inc., 1969
Godden, Geoffrey A.
    Minton Pottery and Porcelain of the
        First Period, 1793–1850
    London: Herbert Jenkins, 1968
Hobson, R. L.
    Catalogue of the Frank Lloyd Collection
        of Worcester Porcelain of the
        Dr. Wall Period
    London: The British Museum, 1923
Hurlbutt, Frank
    Bow Porcelain
    London: G. Bell and Sons, 1926
John, W. D.
    Nantgarw Porcelain
    Newport, Monmouthshire, England: R. H. Johns, Ltd., 1948
Lane, Arthur
    English Porcelain Figures of the 18th
        Century
    New York: Thomas Yoseloff, 1961
MacKenna, F. Severne
    Chelsea Porcelain: The Gold Anchor Wares
    Leigh-on-Sea, Essex, England: F. Lewis Publishers, Ltd., 1948

MacKenna, F. Severne
Chelsea Porcelain: The Red Anchor Period
Leigh-on-Sea, Essex, England: F. Lewis Publishers, Ltd., 1948
MacKenna, F. Severne
Chelsea Porcelain: The Triangle and Raised Anchor Wares
Leigh-on-Sea, Essex, England: F. Lewis Publishers, Ltd., 1948
MacKenna, F. Severne
Cookworthy's Plymouth and Bristol Porcelain
Leigh-on-Sea, Essex, England: F. Lewis Publishers, Ltd., 1947
MacKenna, F. Severne
Worcester Porcelain: The Wall Period and Its Antecedents
Leigh-on-Sea, Essex, England: F. Lewis Publishers, Ltd., 1950
Mankowitz, Wolf, and Reginald G. Haggar
*The Concise Encyclopedia of English Pottery
and Porcelain*
New York: Hawthorn Books, Inc., 1957
Marshall, H. Rissik
*Coloured Worcester Porcelain of the First
Period (1751–83)*
Newport, Monmouthshire, England: Ceramic Book Company, 1954
Nance, E. Morton
*The Pottery and Porcelain of Swansea
and Nantgarw*
London: B. T. Batsford, Ltd., 1942
Rackham, Bernard, ed.
Catalogue of the Schreiber Collection, vol. 1, *Porcelain*
London: Victoria and Albert Museum, 1928
Sandon, Henry
The Illustrated Guide to Worcester Porcelain (1751–1793)
London: Herbert Jenkins (n.d.)
Savage, George
18th Century English Porcelain
New York: The Macmillan Company, 1952
Savage, George
English Pottery and Porcelain
New York: Universe Books, 1961
Tudor-Craig, Sir Algernon
Armorial Porcelain of the Eighteenth Century
London: The Century House, 1925

OTHER REFERENCES

Syz, Hans
"Some Oriental Aspects of European
Ceramic Decoration"
Antiques Magazine, May and July, 1969
Barber, Edwin A.
*The Pottery and Porcelain of the
United States,* 2d ed., rev.
New York: G. P. Putnam's Sons, 1901
Beurdeley, Michel
"The China That Came from Japan"
Réalités, May, 1970, English-language edition

Hood, Graham
Bonnin and Morris of Philadelphia
The First American Porcelain Factory, 1770–1772
Pub. for the Institute of Early American History and Culture
at Williamsburg, Virginia
The University of North Carolina Press, Chapel Hill, 1972

Several periodicals regularly publish special articles in the field of antique porcelain. These include:
The Antique Collector, Antiques Magazine (American), *Apollo, Collector's Guide, Connoisseur.* Also *Transactions of the English Ceramic Circle.*

Auction houses regularly conducting sales of antique porcelain publish catalogues of the sales and, later, lists of prices paid. One may subscribe to both. Two leading auction houses are:

Christie, Manson and Woods
8 King Street, St. James, London S.W. 1
Porcelain sales on Mondays

Sotheby, Parke Bernet, Inc.
34–35 New Bond Street, London, W. 1
Porcelain sales on Tuesdays

980 Madison Avenue, New York, N.Y. 10021
Periodic sales of porcelains, with advance exhibitions and printed catalogues.

Also useful as references for auctions, fairs, and dealers in antique porcelain: *The International Antiques Yearbook* (published in September) and the *British Antique Yearbook* (published in April), Apollo Magazine Publications, Ltd., 22 Davis Street, London. Both sold in the U.S.A.

Museum guides include *The Directory of Museums* (U.S.), published annually, and *Museums and Galleries of Great Britain and Ireland,* published annually in England by Index Publications, London Road, Dunstable, Bedfordshire.

Sources of ultraviolet equipment include:
Ultraviolet Light Products
San Gabriel, California
(UVSL-25 "Mineralight")

Arthur H. Thomas
Box 779
Philadelphia, Pennsylvania 19105
(Long- and Short-Wave Ultraviolet Lamps)

Harshaw Scientific
Jackson and Swanson Streets
Philadelphia, Pennsylvania 19148
(Short- and Long-Range Ultraviolet Lamps)

PUBLIC COLLECTIONS OF
ANTIQUE PORCELAIN

UNITED STATES

Baltimore, Md.	Walters Art Gallery	Chinese, English, Sèvres
Boston, Mass.	Museum of Fine Arts	Chinese, Chinese Export, Continental, English
Brooklyn, N.Y.	Brooklyn Museum	English, Continental
Camden, N.J.	The Campbell Museum	General
Charlotte, N.C.	Mint Museum of Art	English, Continental
Chicago, Ill.	Art Institute of Chicago	Chinese, Continental, English
Cincinnati, Ohio	Taft Museum	American, Chinese
Cleveland, Ohio	Cleveland Museum of Art	Chinese, Continental
Dearborn, Mich.	Henry Ford Museum	American, English
Detroit, Mich.	Detroit Institute of Arts	Continental, English
Harrisburg, Pa.	William Penn Memorial Museum	Tucker (American)
Hartford, Conn.	Wadsworth Atheneum	French, German
Jacksonville, Fla.	Cummer Gallery of Art	Meissen
Kansas City, Mo.	Nelson Gallery	Chinese
Los Angeles, Calif.	Los Angeles County Museum	Chinese Export, Continental
Newark, N.J.	Newark Museum	American, English
New York, N.Y.	Hispanic Society of America	Italian, Spanish
	Metropolitan Museum of Art	American, Chinese, Chinese Export, Continental, English
	Cooper-Hewitt Museum	Continental, English
Philadelphia, Pa.	Philadelphia Museum of Art	American, Chinese, Continental
Providence, R.I.	Museum, Rhode Island School of Design	Chinese, European
Saint Louis, Mo.	City Art Museum	Continental
San Francisco, Calif.	DeYoung Memorial Museum	Chinese, Continental, English, French, Japanese
	Palace of Legion of Honor	
San Marino, Calif.	Huntington Library	Chelsea, Chinese
Salem, Mass.	Peabody Museum	Chinese Export, Liverpool
Seattle, Wash.	Seattle Art Museum	Continental
Shelburne, Vt.	Shelburne Museum	Chinese, English
Washington, D.C.	Freer Gallery of Art	Oriental
	National Gallery of Art	Chinese

142

	National Museum of History and Technology (Smithsonian Institution)	Continental, English
Williamsburg, Va.	Colonial Williamsburg Museum	English
Winterthur, Del.	Henry Francis du Pont Winterthur Museum	Chinese Export, English

GREAT BRITAIN

Aylesbury, Buckingham	Waddesdon Manor	French
Bedford	Cecil Higgins Art Gallery	Continental, English
Bedfordshire	Luton Hoo House	English
Birkenhead, Cheshire	Williamson Art Gallery and Museum	Liverpool
Brighton	The Royal Pavilion Art Gallery and Museum	English
Bristol	Bristol City Art Gallery	English
Cambridge	Fitzwilliam Museum	English
Cardiff, Wales	National Museum of Wales	Welsh
Cheltenham, Gloucestershire	Cheltenham Art Gallery and Museum	English
Derby	Museum and Art Gallery	Derby
Liverpool	Liverpool Museum	Liverpool
London	British Museum	All porcelains
	Victoria and Albert Museum	Chinese, Continental, English
	Percival David Foundation	Chinese
	Wallace Collection	French, especially Sèvres
Oxford	Ashmolean Museum	Worcester
Oxfordshire	Blenheim Palace	Chinese
Stoke-on-Trent	City Museum and Art Gallery	English
Swansea, Wales	Glynn Vivian Art Gallery	Nangarw, Swansea
Worcester	Worcester Works Museum	Dyson Perrins Collection

THE CONTINENT

Amsterdam, The Netherlands	Rijksmuseum	Dutch, Meissen, Oriental
Berlin (West), Germany	Kunstgewerbemuseum	German
	Porzellansammlung der Staatlichen Porzellanmanufaktur	Berlin

Bruges, Belgium	Gruuthusemuseum	Continental, Oriental
Brussels, Belgium	Historical Museum, Maison du Roi	General collection
	Musées de la Cinquantenaire	Chinese, Tournai
Darmstadt, W. Germany	Grossherzogliche Porzellansammlung im Prinz-Georg-Palais	Kelsterbach
Düsseldorf, W. Germany	Kunstmuseum der Stadt Düsseldorf	German
Dresden, E. Germany	Zwinger Museum	Meissen
Gothenburg, Sweden	Historiska Museet	Chinese Export
Hamburg, W. Germany	Museum für Kunst und Gewerbe	Meissen, Oriental
Istanbul, Turkey	Topkapu Sarayi Müzesi	Chinese (Ming)
Köln, W. Germany	Kunstgewerbemuseum	German
Liège, Belgium	Museum of Mariemont	Tournai
Lisbon, Portugal	Espirito Santo Collection	Chinese Export
Madrid, Spain	Royal Palace, Aranjuez	Buen Retiro, Italian
Munich, W. Germany	Bayerisches Nationalmuseum	Meissen, Nymphenburg
	Residenzmuseum	Nymphenburg
Naples, Italy	Capodimonte Museum	Italian
Paris, France	Musée des Arts Décoratifs	French
Saarbrücken, W. Germany	Saarlandmuseum	German
Sèvres, France	Musée National de Céramique	Sèvres

OTHER MUSEUMS

Leningrad, U.S.S.R.	Hermitage Museum	French, Russian
Manila, The Philippines	Manila Museum	Chinese
Singapore	Singapore Museum	Chinese
Taipei, Taiwan	National Palace Museum	Chinese
Tehran, Iran	Archeological Museum	Chinese
Toronto, Canada	Royal Ontario Museum	Chinese

NOTE: The porcelains listed for each museum are those most important or dominant in the collection. Nearly every large city offers representative museum collections of antique porcelain, especially that produced in the local area or country. Examples include Tokyo, Vienna, Stockholm, and Edinburgh.